Federal Bureau of Investigation

Washington, D.C. 20535

November 1, 2019

MR. JASON LEOPOLD
BUZZFEED
C/O MERRICK JASON WAYNE
MATTHEW TOPIC
LOEVY & LOEVY
THIRD FLOOR
311 N. ABERDEN STREET
CHICAGO, IL 60607

> FOIPA Request No.: 1432673-000
> Civil Action No.: 19-cv-01278
> Subject: All 302's of individuals who were
> questioned/interviewed by FBI Agents working for the
> Office of Special Counsel Robert Mueller

Dear Mr. Leopold:

The enclosed documents were reviewed under the Freedom of Information/Privacy Acts (FOIPA), Title 5, United States Code, Section 552/552a. Below you will find checked boxes under applicable statutes for the exemptions asserted to protect information exempt from disclosure. The appropriate exemptions are noted on the processed pages next to redacted information. In addition, a deleted page information sheet was inserted to indicate where pages were withheld entirely pursuant to applicable exemptions. An Explanation of Exemptions is enclosed to further explain justification for withheld information.

Section 552		Section 552a
☑ (b)(1)	☑ (b)(7)(A)	☐ (d)(5)
☐ (b)(2)	☑ (b)(7)(B)	☐ (j)(2)
☑ (b)(3)	☑ (b)(7)(C)	☐ (k)(1)
Federal Rules of	☐ (b)(7)(D)	☐ (k)(2)
Criminal Procedure 6(e)	☑ (b)(7)(E)	☐ (k)(3)
50 U.S.C § 3024(i)	☐ (b)(7)(F)	☐ (k)(4)
☐ (b)(4)	☐ (b)(8)	☐ (k)(5)
☑ (b)(5)	☐ (b)(9)	☐ (k)(6)
☑ (b)(6)		☐ (k)(7)

503 pages were reviewed and 266 pages are being released.

☑ Deletions were made by the Department of Justice/Office of Information Policy . To appeal those denials, please write directly to that agency.

Please see the paragraphs below for relevant information specific to your request and the enclosed FBI FOIPA Addendum for standard responses applicable to all requests.

☑ Document(s) were located which originated with, or contained information concerning, other Government Agency (ies) [OGA].

☐ This information has been referred to the OGA(s) for review and direct response to you.
☑ We are consulting with another agency. The FBI will correspond with you regarding this information when the consultation is completed.

Please refer to the enclosed FBI FOIPA Addendum for additional standard responses applicable to your request. **"Part 1"** of the Addendum includes standard responses that apply to all requests. **"Part 2"** includes additional standard responses that apply to all requests for records on individuals. **"Part 3"** includes general information about FBI records that you may find useful. Also enclosed is our Explanation of Exemptions.

Although your request is in litigation, we are required by law to provide you the following information:

You may file an appeal by writing to the Director, Office of Information Policy (OIP), United States Department of Justice, Sixth Floor, 441 G Street, NW, Washington, D.C. 20001, or you may submit an appeal through OIP's FOIA online portal by creating an account on the following website: https://www.foiaonline.gov/foiaonline/action/public/home. Your appeal must be postmarked or electronically transmitted within ninety (90) days from the date of this letter in order to be considered timely. If you submit your appeal by mail, both the letter and the envelope should be clearly marked "Freedom of Information Act Appeal." Please cite the FOIPA Request Number assigned to your request so it may be easily identified.

You may seek dispute resolution services by contacting the Office of Government Information Services (OGIS). The contact information for OGIS is as follows: Office of Government Information Services, National Archives and Records Administration, 8601 Adelphi Road-OGIS, College Park, Maryland 20740-6001, e-mail at ogis@nara.gov; telephone at 202-741-5770; toll free at 1-877-684-6448; or facsimile at 202-741-5769. Alternatively, you may contact the FBI's FOIA Public Liaison by emailing foipaquestions@fbi.gov. If you submit your dispute resolution correspondence by email, the subject heading should clearly state "Dispute Resolution Services." Please also cite the FOIPA Request Number assigned to your request so it may be easily identified.

Please direct any further inquiries about this case to the Attorney representing the Government in this matter. Please use the FOIPA Request Number and/or Civil Action Number in all correspondence or inquiries concerning your request.

☑ See additional information which follows.

Sincerely,

David M. Hardy
Section Chief
Record/Information
  Dissemination Section
Information Management Division

Enclosures

Additional Information:

In response to your Freedom of Information/Privacy Acts (FOIPA) request, enclosed is a processed copy of Bates Stamped documents, FBI (19-cv-1278)-1 through FBI (19-cv-1278)-503. The enclosed documents represent the first interim release of information responsive to your request. To minimize costs to both you and the FBI, duplicate copies of the same document were not processed.

FBI FOIPA Addendum

As referenced in our letter responding to your Freedom of Information/Privacy Acts (FOIPA) request, the FBI FOIPA Addendum includes information applicable to your request. Part 1 of the Addendum includes standard responses that apply to all requests. Part 2 includes additional standard responses that apply to all requests for records on individuals. Part 3 includes general information about FBI records. For questions regarding Parts 1, 2, or 3, visit the www.fbi.gov/foia website under "Contact Us." Previously mentioned appeal and dispute resolution services are also available at the web address.

Part 1: The standard responses below apply to all requests:

(i) **5 U.S.C. § 552(c).** Congress excluded three categories of law enforcement and national security records from the requirements of the FOIA [5 U.S.C. § 552(c) (2006 & Supp. IV (2010)]. FBI responses are limited to those records subject to the requirements of the FOIA. Additional information about the FBI and the FOIPA can be found on the www.fbi.gov/foia website.

(ii) **National Security/Intelligence Records.** The FBI can neither confirm nor deny the existence of national security and foreign intelligence records pursuant to FOIA exemptions (b)(1), (b)(3), and PA exemption (j)(2) as applicable to requests for records about individuals [5 U.S.C. §§ 552/552a (b)(1), (b)(3), and (j)(2); 50 U.S.C § 3024(i)(1)]. The mere acknowledgment of the existence or nonexistence of such records is itself a classified fact protected by FOIA exemption (b)(1) and/or would reveal intelligence sources, methods, or activities protected by exemption (b)(3) [50 USC § 3024(i)(1)]. This is a standard response and should not be read to indicate that national security or foreign intelligence records do or do not exist.

Part 2: The standard responses below apply to all requests for records on individuals:

(i) **Requests for Records about any Individual—Watch Lists.** The FBI can neither confirm nor deny the existence of any individual's name on a watch list pursuant to FOIA exemption (b)(7)(E) and PA exemption (j)(2) [5 U.S.C. §§ 552/552a (b)(7)(E), (j)(2)]. This is a standard response and should not be read to indicate that watch list records do or do not exist.

(ii) **Requests for Records for Incarcerated Individuals.** The FBI can neither confirm nor deny the existence of records which could reasonably be expected to endanger the life or physical safety of any incarcerated individual pursuant to FOIA exemptions (b)(7)(E), (b)(7)(F), and PA exemption (j)(2) [5 U.S.C. §§ 552/552a (b)(7)(E), (b)(7)(F), and (j)(2)]. This is a standard response and should not be read to indicate that such records do or do not exist.

Part 3: General Information:

(i) **Record Searches.** The Record/Information Dissemination Section (RIDS) searches for reasonably described records by searching those systems or locations where responsive records would reasonably be found. A reasonable search normally consists of a search for main files in the Central Records System (CRS), an extensive system of records consisting of applicant, investigative, intelligence, personnel, administrative, and general files compiled and maintained by the FBI in the course of fulfilling law enforcement, intelligence, and administrative functions. The CRS spans the entire FBI organization and encompasses the records of FBI Headquarters (FBIHQ), FBI Field Offices, and FBI Legal Attaché Offices (Legats) worldwide and includes Electronic Surveillance (ELSUR) records. For additional information about our record searches visit www.fbi.gov/services/information-management/foipa/requesting-fbi-records.

(ii) **FBI Records.** Founded in 1908, the FBI carries out a dual law enforcement and national security mission. As part of this dual mission, the FBI creates and maintains records on various subjects; however, the FBI does not maintain records on every person, subject, or entity.

(iii) **Requests for Criminal History Records or Rap Sheets.** The Criminal Justice Information Services (CJIS) Division provides Identity History Summary Checks – often referred to as a criminal history record or rap sheets. These criminal history records are not the same as material in an investigative "FBI file." An Identity History Summary Check is a listing of information taken from fingerprint cards and documents submitted to the FBI in connection with arrests, federal employment, naturalization, or military service. For a fee, individuals can request a copy of their Identity History Summary Check. Forms and directions can be accessed at www.fbi.gov/about-us/cjis/identity-history-summary-checks. Additionally, requests can be submitted electronically at www.edo.cjis.gov. For additional information, please contact CJIS directly at (304) 625-5590.

(iv) **The National Name Check Program (NNCP).** The mission of NNCP is to analyze and report information in response to name check requests received from federal agencies, for the purpose of protecting the United States from foreign and domestic threats to national security. Please be advised that this is a service provided to other federal agencies. Private citizens cannot request a name check.

EXPLANATION OF EXEMPTIONS

SUBSECTIONS OF TITLE 5, UNITED STATES CODE, SECTION 552

(b)(1) (A) specifically authorized under criteria established by an Executive order to be kept secret in the interest of national defense or foreign policy and (B) are in fact properly classified to such Executive order;

(b)(2) related solely to the internal personnel rules and practices of an agency;

(b)(3) specifically exempted from disclosure by statute (other than section 552b of this title), provided that such statute (A) requires that the matters be withheld from the public in such a manner as to leave no discretion on issue, or (B) establishes particular criteria for withholding or refers to particular types of matters to be withheld;

(b)(4) trade secrets and commercial or financial information obtained from a person and privileged or confidential;

(b)(5) inter-agency or intra-agency memorandums or letters which would not be available by law to a party other than an agency in litigation with the agency;

(b)(6) personnel and medical files and similar files the disclosure of which would constitute a clearly unwarranted invasion of personal privacy;

(b)(7) records or information compiled for law enforcement purposes, but only to the extent that the production of such law enforcement records or information (A) could reasonably be expected to interfere with enforcement proceedings, (B) would deprive a person of a right to a fair trial or an impartial adjudication, (C) could reasonably be expected to constitute an unwarranted invasion of personal   privacy, (D) could reasonably be expected to disclose the identity of confidential source, including a State, local, or foreign agency or authority or any private institution which furnished information on a confidential basis, and, in the case of record or information compiled by a criminal law enforcement authority in the course of a criminal investigation, or by an agency conducting a lawful national security intelligence investigation, information furnished by a confidential source, (E) would disclose techniques and procedures for law enforcement investigations or prosecutions, or would disclose guidelines for law enforcement investigations or prosecutions if such disclosure could reasonably be expected to risk circumvention of the law, or (F) could reasonably be expected to endanger the life or physical safety of any individual;

(b)(8) contained in or related to examination, operating, or condition reports prepared by, on behalf of, or for the use of an agency responsible for the regulation or supervision of financial institutions; or

(b)(9) geological and geophysical information and data, including maps, concerning wells.

SUBSECTIONS OF TITLE 5, UNITED STATES CODE, SECTION 552a

(d)(5) information compiled in reasonable anticipation of a civil action proceeding;

(j)(2) material reporting investigative efforts pertaining to the enforcement of criminal law including efforts to prevent, control,   or reduce crime or apprehend criminals;

(k)(1) information which is currently and properly classified pursuant to an Executive order in the interest of the national defense or foreign policy, for example, information involving intelligence sources or methods;

(k)(2) investigatory material compiled for law enforcement purposes, other than criminal, which did not result in loss of a right, benefit or privilege under Federal programs, or which would identify a source who furnished information pursuant to a promise that his/her identity would be held in confidence;

(k)(3) material maintained in connection with providing protective services to the President of the United States or any other individual pursuant to the authority of Title 18, United States Code, Section 3056;

(k)(4) required by statute to be maintained and used solely as statistical records;

(k)(5) investigatory material compiled solely for the purpose of determining suitability, eligibility, or qualifications for Federal civilian employment or for access to classified information, the disclosure of which would reveal the identity of the person who furnished information pursuant to a promise that his/her identity would be held in confidence;

(k)(6) testing or examination material used to determine individual qualifications for appointment or promotion in Federal Government service the release of which would compromise the testing or examination process;

(k)(7) material used to determine potential for promotion in the armed services, the disclosure of which would reveal the identity of the person who furnished the material pursuant to a promise that his/her identity would be held in confidence.

FEDERAL BUREAU OF INVESTIGATION
FOI/PA
DELETED PAGE INFORMATION SHEET
Civil Action No.: 19-cv-1278 / 19-cv-1626
FOIA: 1432673-000 / 1433273-000
PDF Title: 19-cv-1278 Release 1 Bates 1-503

Total Withheld Pages = 237

Bates Page Reference	Reason for Withholding (i.e., exemptions with coded rationale, duplicate, sealed by order of court, etc.)
FBI(19cv1278) 8	b6; b7A; b7B per DOJ/OIP; b7C
FBI(19cv1278) 41	b6; b7A; b7B per DOJ/OIP; b7C
FBI(19cv1278) 44	b6; b7A; b7B per DOJ/OIP; b7C
FBI(19cv1278) 48	b6; b7A; b7B per DOJ/OIP; b7C
FBI(19cv1278) 79	b5 per DOJ/OIP; b6; b7A; b7C
FBI(19cv1278) 80	b5 per DOJ/OIP; b6; b7C
FBI(19cv1278) 81	b5 per DOJ/OIP; b6; b7C
FBI(19cv1278) 84	b5 per DOJ/OIP
FBI(19cv1278) 88	b5 per DOJ/OIP; b6; b7C
FBI(19cv1278) 89	b5 per DOJ/OIP; b6; b7C
FBI(19cv1278) 93	b5 per DOJ/OIP; b6; b7C
FBI(19cv1278) 94	b5 per DOJ/OIP; b6; b7C
FBI(19cv1278) 95	b5 per DOJ/OIP; b6; b7A; b7B per DOJ/OIP; b7C
FBI(19cv1278) 97	b5 per DOJ/OIP; b6; b7A; b7B per DOJ/OIP; b7C
FBI(19cv1278) 98	b5 per DOJ/OIP; b6; b7A; b7B per DOJ/OIP; b7C
FBI(19cv1278) 99	b5 per DOJ/OIP
FBI(19cv1278) 101	b5 per DOJ/OIP
FBI(19cv1278) 102	b5 per DOJ/OIP
FBI(19cv1278) 103	b5 per DOJ/OIP; b6; b7C
FBI(19cv1278) 104	b5 per DOJ/OIP; b6; b7A; b7B per DOJ/OIP; b7C
FBI(19cv1278) 105	b5 per DOJ/OIP; b6; b7A; b7B per DOJ/OIP; b7C
FBI(19cv1278) 106	b5 per DOJ/OIP; b6; b7A; b7B per DOJ/OIP; b7C
FBI(19cv1278) 107	b5 per DOJ/OIP; b6; b7A; b7B per DOJ/OIP; b7C
FBI(19cv1278) 108	b5 per DOJ/OIP; b6; b7A; b7B per DOJ/OIP; b7C
FBI(19cv1278) 109	b5 per DOJ/OIP; b6; b7A; b7B per DOJ/OIP; b7C

XXXXXXXXXXXXXXXXXXXXXXX
X   Deleted Page(s)   X
X   No Duplication Fee X
X   For this Page   X
XXXXXXXXXXXXXXXXXXXXXXX

Bates Page Reference	Reason for Withholding (i.e., exemptions with coded rationale, duplicate, sealed by order of court, etc.)
FBI(19cv1278) 110	b5 per DOJ/OIP; b6; b7A; b7B per DOJ/OIP; b7C
FBI(19cv1278) 111	b5 per DOJ/OIP; b6; b7C
FBI(19cv1278) 112	b5 per DOJ/OIP; b6; b7C
FBI(19cv1278) 113	b7A; b6; b7C
FBI(19cv1278) 114	b5 per DOJ/OIP; b6; b7A; b7C
FBI(19cv1278) 115	b5 per DOJ/OIP; b6; b7A; b7C
FBI(19cv1278) 116	b5 per DOJ/OIP; b6; b7A; b7C
FBI(19cv1278) 117	b5 per DOJ/OIP; b6; b7C
FBI(19cv1278) 118	b5 per DOJ/OIP; b6; b7C
FBI(19cv1278) 119	b5 per DOJ/OIP; b6; b7C
FBI(19cv1278) 120	b5 per DOJ/OIP; b6; b7C
FBI(19cv1278) 121	b5 per DOJ/OIP; b6; b7C
FBI(19cv1278) 122	b5 per DOJ/OIP; b6; b7C
FBI(19cv1278) 123	b5 per DOJ/OIP; b6; b7C
FBI(19cv1278) 124	b5 per DOJ/OIP; b6; b7C
FBI(19cv1278) 125	b5 per DOJ/OIP
FBI(19cv1278) 126	b5 per DOJ/OIP; b6; b7C; b7E
FBI(19cv1278) 127	b5 per DOJ/OIP; b6; b7C; b7E
FBI(19cv1278) 128	b5 per DOJ/OIP; b6; b7C; b7E
FBI(19cv1278) 170	b5 per DOJ/OIP
FBI(19cv1278) 171	b5 per DOJ/OIP
FBI(19cv1278) 172	b5 per DOJ/OIP
FBI(19cv1278) 173	b5 per DOJ/OIP; b6; b7C
FBI(19cv1278) 174	b5 per DOJ/OIP
FBI(19cv1278) 175	b5 per DOJ/OIP
FBI(19cv1278) 180	b5 per DOJ/OIP
FBI(19cv1278) 181	b5 per DOJ/OIP
FBI(19cv1278) 182	b5 per DOJ/OIP
FBI(19cv1278) 183	b5 per DOJ/OIP
FBI(19cv1278) 184	b5 per DOJ/OIP; b6; b7C
FBI(19cv1278) 185	b5 per DOJ/OIP; b6; b7C

```
XXXXXXXXXXXXXXXXXXXXXXX
X    Deleted Page(s)      X
X    No Duplication Fee  X
X    For this Page        X
XXXXXXXXXXXXXXXXXXXXXXX
```

Bates Page Reference	Reason for Withholding (i.e., exemptions with coded rationale, duplicate, sealed by order of court, etc.)
FBI(19cv1278) 187	b5 per DOJ/OIP
FBI(19cv1278) 188	b5 per DOJ/OIP
FBI(19cv1278) 191	b5 per DOJ/OIP
FBI(19cv1278) 192	b5 per DOJ/OIP
FBI(19cv1278) 193	b5 per DOJ/OIP
FBI(19cv1278) 195	b5 per DOJ/OIP; b6; b7C
FBI(19cv1278) 196	b5 per DOJ/OIP
FBI(19cv1278) 197	b5 per DOJ/OIP; b6; b7C
FBI(19cv1278) 198	b5 per DOJ/OIP
FBI(19cv1278) 213	b5 per DOJ/OIP; b6; b7C
FBI(19cv1278) 215	b5 per DOJ/OIP
FBI(19cv1278) 216	Referral/Consult; b3; b5 per DOJ/OIP; b6; b7A per DOJ/OIP; b7C
FBI(19cv1278) 217	Referral/Consult; b3; b5 per DOJ/OIP; b7A per DOJ/OIP
FBI(19cv1278) 218	b6; b7A per DOJ/OIP; b7C
FBI(19cv1278) 220	b5 per DOJ/OIP; b6; b7C
FBI(19cv1278) 236	b6; b7A; b7B per DOJ/OIP; b7C
FBI(19cv1278) 242	b5 per DOJ/OIP; b6; b7C
FBI(19cv1278) 243	b5 per DOJ/OIP; b6; b7C
FBI(19cv1278) 244	b5 per DOJ/OIP; b6; b7C
FBI(19cv1278) 245	b5 per DOJ/OIP; b6; b7C
FBI(19cv1278) 246	b5 per DOJ/OIP; b6; b7C
FBI(19cv1278) 247	b5 per DOJ/OIP; b6; b7C
FBI(19cv1278) 248	b5 per DOJ/OIP; b6; b7C
FBI(19cv1278) 249	b5 per DOJ/OIP; b6; b7C
FBI(19cv1278) 250	b5 per DOJ/OIP; b6; b7C
FBI(19cv1278) 251	b5 per DOJ/OIP; b6; b7C
FBI(19cv1278) 252	b5 per DOJ/OIP; b6; b7C
FBI(19cv1278) 253	b5 per DOJ/OIP; b6; b7C
FBI(19cv1278) 254	b5 per DOJ/OIP; b6; b7C
FBI(19cv1278) 255	b5 per DOJ/OIP; b6; b7C

```
XXXXXXXXXXXXXXXXXXXXXX
X    Deleted Page(s)     X
X    No Duplication Fee X
X    For this Page       X
XXXXXXXXXXXXXXXXXXXXXX
```

Bates Page Reference	Reason for Withholding (i.e., exemptions with coded rationale, duplicate, sealed by order of court, etc.)
FBI(19cv1278) 256	b5 per DOJ/OIP; b6; b7C
FBI(19cv1278) 257	b5 per DOJ/OIP; b6; b7C
FBI(19cv1278) 258	b5 per DOJ/OIP; b6; b7C
FBI(19cv1278) 259	b5 per DOJ/OIP; b6; b7C
FBI(19cv1278) 260	b5 per DOJ/OIP; b6; b7C
FBI(19cv1278) 261	b5 per DOJ/OIP; b6; b7C
FBI(19cv1278) 262	b5 per DOJ/OIP; b6; b7C
FBI(19cv1278) 263	b5 per DOJ/OIP; b6; b7C
FBI(19cv1278) 264	b5 per DOJ/OIP; b6; b7C
FBI(19cv1278) 265	b5 per DOJ/OIP; b6; b7C
FBI(19cv1278) 266	b5 per DOJ/OIP; b6; b7C
FBI(19cv1278) 267	b5 per DOJ/OIP; b6; b7C
FBI(19cv1278) 268	b5 per DOJ/OIP; b6; b7C
FBI(19cv1278) 269	b5 per DOJ/OIP; b6; b7C
FBI(19cv1278) 270	b5 per DOJ/OIP; b6; b7C
FBI(19cv1278) 271	b5 per DOJ/OIP; b6; b7C
FBI(19cv1278) 272	b5 per DOJ/OIP; b6; b7C
FBI(19cv1278) 273	b5 per DOJ/OIP; b6; b7C
FBI(19cv1278) 274	b5 per DOJ/OIP; b6; b7C
FBI(19cv1278) 275	b5 per DOJ/OIP; b6; b7C
FBI(19cv1278) 276	b5 per DOJ/OIP; b6; b7C
FBI(19cv1278) 277	b5 per DOJ/OIP; b6; b7C
FBI(19cv1278) 278	b5 per DOJ/OIP; b6; b7C
FBI(19cv1278) 279	b5 per DOJ/OIP; b6; b7C
FBI(19cv1278) 280	b5 per DOJ/OIP; b6; b7C
FBI(19cv1278) 281	b5 per DOJ/OIP; b6; b7C
FBI(19cv1278) 282	b5 per DOJ/OIP; b6; b7C
FBI(19cv1278) 283	b5 per DOJ/OIP; b6; b7C
FBI(19cv1278) 284	b5 per DOJ/OIP; b6; b7C
FBI(19cv1278) 285	b5 per DOJ/OIP; b6; b7C
FBI(19cv1278) 288	b5 per DOJ/OIP; b6; b7C

Bates Page Reference	Reason for Withholding (i.e., exemptions with coded rationale, duplicate, sealed by order of court, etc.)
FBI(19cv1278) 289	b5 per DOJ/OIP; b6; b7C
FBI(19cv1278) 299	Duplicate
FBI(19cv1278) 300	Duplicate
FBI(19cv1278) 301	Duplicate
FBI(19cv1278) 302	Duplicate
FBI(19cv1278) 303	Duplicate
FBI(19cv1278) 304	Duplicate
FBI(19cv1278) 305	Duplicate
FBI(19cv1278) 316	b5 per DOJ/OIP; b6; b7C
FBI(19cv1278) 317	b5 per DOJ/OIP; b6; b7C
FBI(19cv1278) 318	b5 per DOJ/OIP; b6; b7C
FBI(19cv1278) 319	b5 per DOJ/OIP; b6; b7C
FBI(19cv1278) 320	b5 per DOJ/OIP; b6; b7C
FBI(19cv1278) 321	b5 per DOJ/OIP; b6; b7C
FBI(19cv1278) 352	b6; b7A; b7B per DOJ/OIP; b7C
FBI(19cv1278) 353	b6; b7A; b7B per DOJ/OIP; b7C
FBI(19cv1278) 354	b6; b7A; b7B per DOJ/OIP; b7C
FBI(19cv1278) 355	b6; b7A; b7B per DOJ/OIP; b7C
FBI(19cv1278) 356	b6; b7A; b7B per DOJ/OIP; b7C
FBI(19cv1278) 359	b6; b7A; b7B per DOJ/OIP; b7C
FBI(19cv1278) 360	b6; b7A; b7B per DOJ/OIP; b7C
FBI(19cv1278) 361	b6; b7A; b7B per DOJ/OIP; b7C
FBI(19cv1278) 362	b6; b7A; b7B per DOJ/OIP; b7C
FBI(19cv1278) 363	b6; b7A; b7B per DOJ/OIP; b7C
FBI(19cv1278) 364	b6; b7A; b7B per DOJ/OIP; b7C
FBI(19cv1278) 365	b6; b7A; b7B per DOJ/OIP; b7C
FBI(19cv1278) 366	b6; b7A; b7B per DOJ/OIP; b7C
FBI(19cv1278) 367	b6; b7A; b7B per DOJ/OIP; b7C
FBI(19cv1278) 368	b6; b7A; b7B per DOJ/OIP; b7C
FBI(19cv1278) 369	b6; b7A; b7B per DOJ/OIP; b7C
FBI(19cv1278) 370	b6; b7A; b7B per DOJ/OIP; b7C

```
XXXXXXXXXXXXXXXXXXXXXXX
X    Deleted Page(s)     X
X    No Duplication Fee X
X    For this Page       X
XXXXXXXXXXXXXXXXXXXXXXX
```

Bates Page Reference	Reason for Withholding (i.e., exemptions with coded rationale, duplicate, sealed by order of court, etc.)
FBI(19cv1278) 371	b6; b7A; b7B per DOJ/OIP; b7C
FBI(19cv1278) 372	b6; b7A; b7B per DOJ/OIP; b7C
FBI(19cv1278) 373	b6; b7A; b7B per DOJ/OIP; b7C
FBI(19cv1278) 374	b6; b7A; b7B per DOJ/OIP; b7C
FBI(19cv1278) 375	b6; b7A; b7B per DOJ/OIP; b7C
FBI(19cv1278) 376	b6; b7A; b7B per DOJ/OIP; b7C
FBI(19cv1278) 377	b6; b7A; b7B per DOJ/OIP; b7C
FBI(19cv1278) 379	b6; b7A; b7B per DOJ/OIP; b7C
FBI(19cv1278) 380	b6; b7A; b7B per DOJ/OIP; b7C
FBI(19cv1278) 382	b6; b7A; b7B per DOJ/OIP; b7C
FBI(19cv1278) 388	b5 per DOJ/OIP; b6; b7C
FBI(19cv1278) 390	b5 per DOJ/OIP; b6; b7C
FBI(19cv1278) 391	b5 per DOJ/OIP; b6; b7C
FBI(19cv1278) 392	b5 per DOJ/OIP; b6; b7C
FBI(19cv1278) 393	b5 per DOJ/OIP; b6; b7C
FBI(19cv1278) 394	b5 per DOJ/OIP; b6; b7C
FBI(19cv1278) 395	b5 per DOJ/OIP; b6; b7C
FBI(19cv1278) 396	b5 per DOJ/OIP; b6; b7C
FBI(19cv1278) 397	b5 per DOJ/OIP; b6; b7C
FBI(19cv1278) 398	b5 per DOJ/OIP; b6; b7C
FBI(19cv1278) 399	b5 per DOJ/OIP; b6; b7C
FBI(19cv1278) 400	b5 per DOJ/OIP; b6; b7C
FBI(19cv1278) 401	b5 per DOJ/OIP; b6; b7C
FBI(19cv1278) 402	b5 per DOJ/OIP; b6; b7C
FBI(19cv1278) 403	b5 per DOJ/OIP; b6; b7C
FBI(19cv1278) 404	b5 per DOJ/OIP; b6; b7C
FBI(19cv1278) 405	b5 per DOJ/OIP; b6; b7C
FBI(19cv1278) 409	Duplicate
FBI(19cv1278) 410	Duplicate
FBI(19cv1278) 411	Duplicate
FBI(19cv1278) 412	Duplicate

```
XXXXXXXXXXXXXXXXXXXXXXX
X    Deleted Page(s)      X
X    No Duplication Fee X
X    For this Page        X
XXXXXXXXXXXXXXXXXXXXXXX
```

Bates Page Reference	Reason for Withholding (i.e., exemptions with coded rationale, duplicate, sealed by order of court, etc.)
FBI(19cv1278) 413	b5 per DOJ/OIP; b6; b7C
FBI(19cv1278) 414	b5 per DOJ/OIP
FBI(19cv1278) 415	b5 per DOJ/OIP
FBI(19cv1278) 416	b5 per DOJ/OIP
FBI(19cv1278) 417	b5 per DOJ/OIP
FBI(19cv1278) 418	b5 per DOJ/OIP
FBI(19cv1278) 419	b5 per DOJ/OIP
FBI(19cv1278) 420	b5 per DOJ/OIP
FBI(19cv1278) 421	b5 per DOJ/OIP
FBI(19cv1278) 422	b5 per DOJ/OIP
FBI(19cv1278) 423	b5 per DOJ/OIP; b6; b7C
FBI(19cv1278) 447	b5 per DOJ/OIP
FBI(19cv1278) 448	b5 per DOJ/OIP; b6; b7C
FBI(19cv1278) 449	b5 per DOJ/OIP; b6; b7C
FBI(19cv1278) 450	b5 per DOJ/OIP; b6; b7C
FBI(19cv1278) 451	b5 per DOJ/OIP
FBI(19cv1278) 452	b5 per DOJ/OIP; b6; b7A; b7C
FBI(19cv1278) 453	b5 per DOJ/OIP
FBI(19cv1278) 455	b5 per DOJ/OIP
FBI(19cv1278) 457	b5 per DOJ/OIP
FBI(19cv1278) 458	b5 per DOJ/OIP
FBI(19cv1278) 459	b5 per DOJ/OIP; b6; b7A; b7C
FBI(19cv1278) 460	b5 per DOJ/OIP; b7A
FBI(19cv1278) 461	b5 per DOJ/OIP; b6; b7C
FBI(19cv1278) 462	b5 per DOJ/OIP
FBI(19cv1278) 463	b5 per DOJ/OIP; b6; b7A; b7B per DOJ/OIP; b7C
FBI(19cv1278) 465	b5 per DOJ/OIP; b6; b7A; b7B per DOJ/OIP; b7C
FBI(19cv1278) 466	b5 per DOJ/OIP; b6; b7A; b7B per DOJ/OIP; b7C
FBI(19cv1278) 467	b5 per DOJ/OIP; b6; b7A; b7B per DOJ/OIP; b7C
FBI(19cv1278) 468	b5 per DOJ/OIP; b6; b7A; b7B per DOJ/OIP; b7C
FBI(19cv1278) 469	b5 per DOJ/OIP; b6; b7A; b7B per DOJ/OIP; b7C

```
XXXXXXXXXXXXXXXXXXXXXXX
X    Deleted Page(s)    X
X    No Duplication Fee X
X    For this Page      X
XXXXXXXXXXXXXXXXXXXXXXX
```

Bates Page Reference	Reason for Withholding (i.e., exemptions with coded rationale, duplicate, sealed by order of court, etc.)
FBI(19cv1278) 470	b5 per DOJ/OIP; b6; b7A; b7B per DOJ/OIP; b7C
FBI(19cv1278) 471	b5 per DOJ/OIP; b6; b7A; b7B per DOJ/OIP; b7C
FBI(19cv1278) 472	b5 per DOJ/OIP; b6; b7C
FBI(19cv1278) 473	b5 per DOJ/OIP; b6; b7C
FBI(19cv1278) 474	b5 per DOJ/OIP
FBI(19cv1278) 475	b5 per DOJ/OIP
FBI(19cv1278) 476	b5 per DOJ/OIP
FBI(19cv1278) 477	b5 per DOJ/OIP
FBI(19cv1278) 478	b5 per DOJ/OIP
FBI(19cv1278) 479	b5 per DOJ/OIP; b6; b7C
FBI(19cv1278) 480	b5 per DOJ/OIP
FBI(19cv1278) 483	b5 per DOJ/OIP
FBI(19cv1278) 484	b5 per DOJ/OIP; b6; b7C
FBI(19cv1278) 485	b5 per DOJ/OIP
FBI(19cv1278) 487	b5 per DOJ/OIP
FBI(19cv1278) 488	b5 per DOJ/OIP; b6; b7C
FBI(19cv1278) 489	b5 per DOJ/OIP; b6; b7A; b7B per DOJ/OIP; b7C
FBI(19cv1278) 490	b5 per DOJ/OIP; b6; b7A; b7C
FBI(19cv1278) 492	b5 per DOJ/OIP; b6; b7C
FBI(19cv1278) 493	b5 per DOJ/OIP; b6; b7C
FBI(19cv1278) 494	b5 per DOJ/OIP; b6; b7C
FBI(19cv1278) 495	b5 per DOJ/OIP; b6; b7C
FBI(19cv1278) 496	b5 per DOJ/OIP
FBI(19cv1278) 497	b5 per DOJ/OIP; b6; b7C
FBI(19cv1278) 498	b5 per DOJ/OIP; b6; b7C
FBI(19cv1278) 499	b5 per DOJ/OIP; b6; b7C
FBI(19cv1278) 500	b5 per DOJ/OIP

```
XXXXXXXXXXXXXXXXXXXXXXX
X    Deleted Page(s)     X
X    No Duplication Fee X
X    For this Page       X
XXXXXXXXXXXXXXXXXXXXXXX
```

FD-302 (Rev. 5-8-10)

b7E

OFFICIAL RECORD

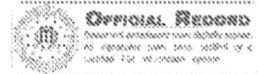

UNCLASSIFIED//~~FOUO~~

FEDERAL BUREAU OF INVESTIGATION

Date of entry   05/10/2018

Richard Gates, was interviewed at 395 E Street SW, Washington, D.C. Present for the interview were SA [   ] ASAC [   ] **b6** **b7C**
[   ] Senior Assistant Special Counsel (SASC) Greg Andres, SASC Jeannie Rhee, SASC Andrew Weissmann, Assistant Special Counsel (ASC) Aaron Zelinsky, and IA [   ] After being advised of the official identities of the interviewing parties and the nature of the interview, Gates provided the following information:

b6
b7A
Gates began the interview by advising [   ] **b7B Per DOJ/OIP**
[   ] were not happy with Gates's cooperation with the Special **b7C**
Counsel's investigation.

[   ]

b6
b7A
b7B Per DOJ/OIP
b7C

b6
b7A
b7B Per DOJ/OIP
b7C

UNCLASSIFIED//~~FOUO~~

Investigation on   04/10/2018   at Washington, District Of Columbia, United States (In Person)

File # [   ]   Date drafted 04/24/2018

by [   ]

b6
b7C
b7E
b7A

FBI(19cv1278)-1

b7E
b7A

UNCLASSIFIED//~~FOUO~~

(U//FOUO) Richard Gates Interview 04/10
Continuation of FD-302 of /2018_____ . On 04/10/2018 . Page 2 of 6

b6
b7A
b7B **Per DOJ/OIP**
b7C

b6
b7A
b7B **Per DOJ/OIP**
b7C

b6
b7A
b7B **Per DOJ/OIP**
b7C

[Note: On 06/12/2016, Assange stated he had
"upcoming leaks in relation to Hillary Clinton... We have emails pending
publication."].

b6
b7A
b7B **Per DOJ/OIP**
b7C

Gates said as of May 2016, h
(Gates) was not aware of the source of the hack.

b6
b7A
b7B **Per DOJ/OIP**
b7C

b6
b7A
b7B **Per DOJ/OIP**
b7C

FD-302a (Rev. 05-08-10)

b7E
b7A

(U//FOUO) Richard Gates Interview 04/10
/2018

Continuation of FD-302 of _____, On 04/10/2018 , Page 3 of 6

b6
b7A
b7B Per DOJ/OIP
b7C

b6
b7A
b7B Per DOJ/OIP
b7C

b6
b7A
b7B Per DOJ/OIP
b7C

b6
b7A
b7B Per DOJ/OIP
b7C

b6
b7A
b7B Per DOJ/OIP
b7C

[Note: On or about 06/27/2016, DNC emails were posted by DCLeaks].

b6
b7A
b7B Per DOJ/OIP
b7C

FBI(19cv1278)-3

UNCLASSIFIED//~~FOUO~~

b7E
b7A

b6
b7A
b7B Per DOJ/OIP
b7C

Campaign Response to Hacked Emails

b6
b7A
b7B Per DOJ/OIP
b7C

Gates said there was also an inside job theory about how the emails were obtained fueled by the death of Seth Rich [Note: Seth Conrad Rich was an employee of the DNC who was fatally shot in Washington, D.C. on 07/10/2016]. Gates said he was never present at any talks suggesting the campaign push the inside job theory. The Trump campaign team also thought the Democrats were pushing the Russia narrative.

Gates said Donald Trump Jr. would ask where the emails were in family meetings. Michael Flynn, Kushner, Manafort, [   ] Lewandowski, Jeff Sessions, and Sam Clovis expressed interest in obtaining the emails as well. Gates said the priority focuses of the Trump campaign opposition research team were Clinton's emails and contributions to the Clinton Foundation. Flynn, [   ] Sessions, Kushner, and Trump Jr. were all focused on opposition topics.

b6
b7C

Gates said interest in the emails was ratcheting up in the April/May 2016 timeframe because it was likely the emails could help Trump's campaign. [

]

b6
b7A
b7B Per DOJ/OIP
b7C

Trump Jr. never communicated anything about the 06/09/2016 meeting with Gates. After the news broke about the 06/09/2016 meeting, Manafort asked Gates if he (Gates) was there. [Note: The 06/09/2016 meeting is a reference to a meeting that took place at Trump Tower arranged on the

UNCLASSIFIED//~~FOUO~~

FD-302a (Rev. 05-08-10)

pretense that documents and information that would incriminate Hillary
Clinton would be provided to the Trump campaign by a Russian government
attorney later identified as Natalia Veselnitskaya]

b6
b7A
b7B Per DOJ/OIP
b7C

Gates said Trump was interested in the emails but remained composed
with a healthy skepticism.

Gates recalled communication with Reince Preibus and [   ] The RNC
was energized by Assange's announcement on 06/12/2016. Gates indicated
that based on a conversation with Manafort, Gates knew the RNC was going
to run the Wikileaks issue to ground, they had more resources to commit to
this effort. Trump and Kushner were initially skeptical about cooperating
with the RNC, but the Wikileaks issue was a turning point.

b6
b7C

Gates described the campaign response to the report as euphoric.

b6
b7C
b7E

Gates said the RNC would put out press releases that would serve to
amplify the Wikileaks releases. The RNC also indicated they knew the
timing of the upcoming releases, Gates did not specify who at the RNC knew
this information. Gates said the only non-public information the RNC had
was related to the timing of the releases.

Gates recalled a time on the campaign aircraft when candidate Trump
said, "get the emails." Flynn said he could use his intelligence sources
to obtain the emails. Flynn was adamant the Russians did not carry out the
hack. To support this theory Flynn advised, based on his experience, the
United States Intelligence Community (USIC) was not capable of figuring it
out. Gates opined that Flynn's assessment of the USIC derived from the
negative way in which Flynn departed the USIC. Gates said Flynn had the
most Russia contacts of anyone on the campaign and was in the best
position to ask for the emails if they were out there.

FD-302a (Rev. 05-08-10)

b7E
b7A

UNCLASSIFIED//FOUO

(U//FOUO) Richard Gates Interview 04/10
Continuation of FD-302 of /2018 _____ , On 04/10/2018 , Page 6 of 6

Gates advised Trump Jr. and Manafort also had contacts with, "Russia types." Gates clarified by saying Manafort's connection with Russians was minimal aside from his relationship with Oleg Deripaska. Gates said Manafort primarily had contacts with Ukrainians. Gates recalled Manafort saying the hack was likely carried out by the Ukrainians, not the Russians, which parroted a narrative Kilimnik often supported. Kilimnik also opined the hack could have been perpetrated by Russian operatives in Ukraine.

Gates said based on prior business dealings, Kushner had the best China contacts. Manafort and Gates had discussions pertaining to Kushner's Chinese contacts. Gates said there were numerous foreign requests to meet Trump after the nomination was secured.

At some point, there was speculation the Mossad might have the emails. Gates said there was never any mention of the Saudis or the Emirates having the emails. Manafort was generally skeptical of any offers of information coming to the campaign's attention.

For example, Gates said there was a group of realtors from Kyrgyzstan claiming to have information that may be of use to the campaign. The information pertained to foreign contributions to the Clinton campaign.

Gates said he never heard about the emails or dirt from George Papadopoulos.

Gates said, during the campaign, Trump and Manafort talked to Sean Hannity in their offices often.

4/10/2018

b6
b7A
b7B Per DOJ/OIP
b7C
b7E

calls me agressin

b6
b7A
b7B Per DOJ/OIP
b7C

6/12/2016: [illegible] (emails)

①

4/10/2018

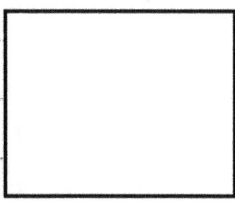

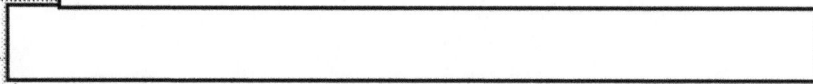

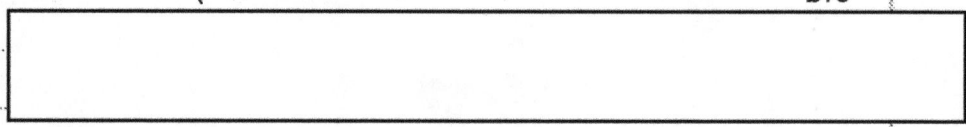

not pleased w RG cooperation

RG not aware in May 2016 source of hack

~ Don Jr. would bring up in family meetings, where are the emails?

FBI(19cv1278)-9

② (circled, top right)

- Flynn, Kushner, Don Jr., PM, [REDACTED] CL, SC, Sessions   b6 b7C b7E
    expressed interest in obtaining emails
- [REDACTED]
- Sessions: Hopefully we can get the emails
- RG did not hear from GP information re: emails/dirt
- April/May ratcheting up of interest bc emails could help campaign
- [REDACTED]

☆ Mid/late May   Sessions/ [REDACTED]

☆   Was walk-ins the only effort to obtain emails ☆   b6 b7A b7B Per DOJ/OIP b7C
☆ · Kyrgyzstan realtors claiming to have information. ✐
  [REDACTED]
· Based on business dealings, JK had best China contacts
        - PM, RG had discussion pertaining to JK Chinese contacts
        - Foreign requests to meet DJT once nomination was secured
· Don Jr had more contacts w/ Russia types, PM as well
        - PM said its probably Ukrainians, not Russians
            - parroted KK's theory
            - KK said it could be Russian operatives in Ukraine

FBI(19cv1278)-10

- At some point, speculation Mossad might have emails
- No mention saudi or UAE might have emails
- Kyrgystan matters offered info re: foreign contributions to HRC
- PM was skeptical of offers of information

b6
b7A
b7B Per DOJ/OIP
b7C

[redacted]

- PM's relationship w/ Russians other than Deripaska was minimal
    - contact was primarily w/ Ukrainians.

[redacted]

- KK told PM it wasn't the Russians, RG said PM didn't follow up

[redacted]

[redacted]

b6
b7A
b7B Per DOJ/OIP
b7C
b7E

- Sense of skepticism re: track record of wiki

[redacted]

- Comms w/ Reince Priebus & [redacted]

b6
b7C

    - RNC was energized by June 12 announcement

④

- RNC was going to run wiki issue to ground, had more resources
  - effort to get emails / materials
  - based on conversation w/ PM
  - DJT & JK skeptical of cooperating w/ RNC, turning point

b6
b7A
b7B Per DOJ/OIP
b7C

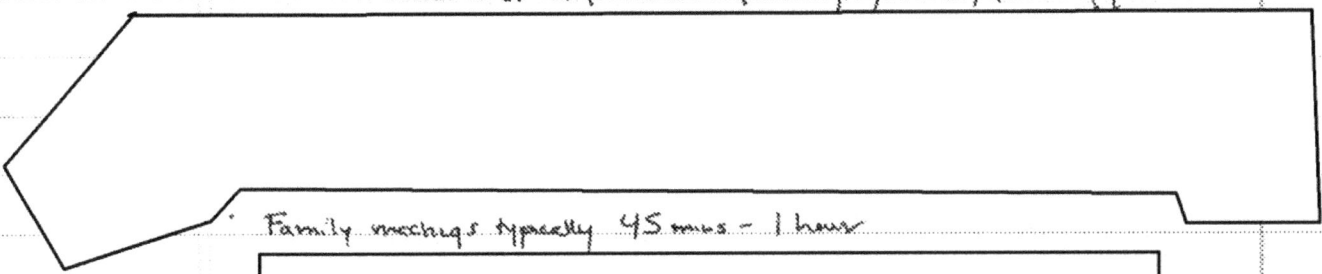

- Family meetings typically 45 mins – 1 hour

- DJT was interested but composed, healthy skepticism
  - PM presented as a first time RNC could help
- RNC put out press releases, amplified Wiki releases
- RNC ~~said~~ indicated they knew timing of upcoming wiki releases
  - RG got info from PM
  - only not public info RNC has is timing of releases
- Flynn says "here is what my intel sources are saying" re: emails
  - talking to candidate
  - why? intel community just not that good
  - never a read out of what Flynn may have obtained
- Inside job theory fueled by Seth Rich death and DWS efforts to minimize and cover up problems. Theory was Dems pushing Russia narrative
- DJT, PM talking to Sean Hannity, in offices quite a bit
- No talks RG was in that suggested pushing inside job theory

or flight

FBI(19cv1278)-12

April 2016

May 18

July 6

- Foreign contrib to CF brought up at June 9 meeting
  (campaign)
  - Emails + CF contrib focus of what camp could use
    - Priority oppo items
- Flynn, [redacted], Sessions, JK, Don Jr. all focused on oppo topics
- Don Jr. never communicated anything about June 9 meeting
  PM, JK

- After news broke, PM asked PG if he was in June 9 meeting

[redacted]

June 2016

[redacted]

7

June 15

June 20

June 23

b6
b7A
b7B Per DOJ/OIP
b7C

(8)

June 27

[redacted]

b6
b7A
b7B Per DOJ/OIP
b7C

· DNC emails posted by DCLeaks

[redacted]

[redacted]

[redacted]

☆ [redacted] ☆

[redacted]

Document ID: 0.7.4249.603642

From:

To: Rick Gates

Cc:

Bcc:

Subject: Gates

Date: Wed Jun 15 2016 17:20:55 EDT

Attachments:

b6
b7C

Still need to talk to u--R.

From:

To:

Subject: Re: Gates

Date: Wed, 15 Jun 2016 21:19:43 +0000

b6
b7C

On Jun 15, 2016, at 5:10 PM,   wrote:

need Jared e-mail...R

From

To:

Subject: Re: Gates

Date: Wed, 15 Jun 2016 20:30:35 +0000

b6
b7C

Jared

On Jun 15, 2016, at 3:30 PM, [   ] wrote:

I need contact infor for [   ]

I need contact info for Jared

R.

FD-302 (Rev. 5-8-10)

b7A
b7E

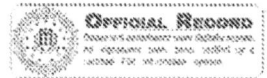

UNCLASSIFIED//~~FOUO~~

FEDERAL BUREAU OF INVESTIGATION

Date of entry   11/20/2018

Richard William Gates III was interviewed was interviewed at 395 E
Street SW, Washington, D.C. Present for the interview were Senior Special
Counsel Attorneys (SASC) Andrew Weissmann and Greg Andres, Assistant
Special Counsel (ASC) Aaron Zelinsky, Special Agent [   ]
[   ] and Intelligence Analyst [   ] Gates's attorney, Tom
Green of Sidley Austin LLP, was also present. After being advised of the
identity of the interviewers and the nature of the interview, Gates
provided the following information:

b6
b7C

b6
b7A
b7B **per DOJ/OIP**
b7C

Gates recalled being in a discussion involving [   ]
Hope Hicks (Hicks), and Manafort. The discussion pertained to the
possibility of [   ] No one on the Donald Trump (Trump)
2016 Presidential campaign (the campaign) team took action on [   ]
[   ]

b6
b7A
b7B **per DOJ/OIP**
b7C

b6
b7C

Gates said there were campaign personnel that thought [   ]
[   ] the missing Clinton server emails. The campaign was planning

b6
b7A
b7B **per DOJ/OIP**
b7C

Investigation on 04/11/2018 at Washington, District Of Columbia, United States (In Person)

File # [   ]   Date drafted 10/16/2018

by [   ]

b6
b7A
b7C
b7E

FBI(19cv1278)-19

FD-302a (Rev. 05-08-10)

b7A
b7E

UNCLASSIFIED//FOUO

(U//FOUO) Interview of Richard Gates 04/11
Continuation of FD-302 of /2018 _____ , On 04/11/2018 , Page 2 of 6

press strategy, a communications campaign, and messaging based on the
possibility the emails existed.

b6
b7A
b7B per DOJ/OIP
b7C

    Gates recalled conversations being held within the campaign about what
the campaign could plan for in the way of emails.

b6
b7A
b7B per DOJ/OIP
b7C

b6
b7A
b7B per DOJ/OIP
b7C

b6
b7A
b7B per DOJ/OIP
b7C

Manafort and Gates were focused on mitigating hit pieces against
Manafort.

b6
b7A
b7B per DOJ/OIP
b7C

June 12, 2016 - July 22, 2016

    Between 06/12/2016 - 07/22/2016
Manafort and Gates   asking when the releases
would happen. Trump was frustrated the releases weren't happening. Gates
said

b6
b7A
b7B per DOJ/OIP
b7C

(U//FOUO) Interview of Richard Gates 04/11
Continuation of FD-302 of /2018   . On 04/11/2018 . Page 3 of 6

b6
b7A
b7B per DOJ/OIP
b7C

Gates said there was a messaging strategy being built around the possible
content of an upcoming release.

Gates indicated there was
disagreement on where the information came from within the campaign. Gates
does not recall Manafort asking Konstantin Kilimnik (Kilimnik) to reach
out to his Russian contacts on the issue, nor did Manafort ask Gates to
call Kilimnik.

b6
b7A
b7B per DOJ/OIP
b7C

Gates said there was also talk about how to clean up Manafort's lawsuit
with Oleg Deripaska (Deripaska) and clean up his image in the media. Gates
said Jared Kushner (Kushner) supported Manafort and that Manafort would
not have lasted without it.

July 22, 2016

Gates said the campaign was very happy about the release by WikiLeaks
on 07/22/2016. Trump was advised not to react to the releases and let it
play out. Gates indicated

b6
b7A
b7B per DOJ/OIP
b7C

and Manafort expressing excitement
there would be additional information coming, however, Gates later said he
did not recall   saying there would be more

Gates said after the WikiLeaks release on 07/22/2016, there was a pivot
to "how do we use the released information"   Gates
reiterated that he did not believe

b6
b7A
b7B per DOJ/OIP
b7C

Gates initially said he did not have
conversations with   after 07/22/2016 about additional information
becoming available,
                                                    after the 07/22
/2016 release.

Late July - 08/19/2016

FD-302a (Rev. 05-08-10)

(U//FOUO) Interview of Richard Gates 04/11
/2018

Continuation of FD-302 of /2018 , On 04/11/2018 , Page 4 of 6

[Agent Note: Manafort resigned from
the campaign on 08/19/2016].

b6
b7A
b7B per DOJ/OIP
b7C

b6
b7A
b7B per DOJ/OIP
b7C

Gates said the campaign was trying to work with the RNC opposition research team.

Gates said Trump's comment "Russia if you're listening" on 07/27/2016 was ad lib.

Gates and Manafort spoke about obtaining the missing emails and Gates understood Manafort   Gates recalled staff meeting conversations about "someone out there has to have the missing emails."

b6
b7A
b7B per DOJ/OIP
b7C

August 2, 2016

Gates recalled that on or about 08/02/2016,

b6
b7A
b7B per DOJ/OIP
b7C

August 2, 2016 - August 21, 2016

b6
b7A
b7B per DOJ/OIP
b7C

FBI(19cv1278)-22

There was
still a more general focus on Clinton's missing emails amongst the
campaign team. Gates said no one used land lines because there were no
walls. Everyone used cell phones.

b6
b7A
b7B per DOJ/OIP
b7C

September 2016

b6
b7A
b7B per DOJ/OIP
b7C

Gates said during September   the upcoming information narrative.
Gates's involvement with the campaign became limited during this timeframe
and he began to work with the "digital folks."

October 4, 2016

b6
b7A
b7B per DOJ/OIP
b7C

October 7, 2016

Gates was not aware of conversations regarding the timing of WikiLeaks
releases approximately 45 minutes after the Access Hollywood tape hit the
media

b6
b7A
b7B per DOJ/OIP
b7C

Rest of October 2016

Gates said the RNC was looking through the releases. The campaign would
pull press releases together based on RNC research and media research.
There was still a pursuit of the missing emails by the campaign.

b6
b7C

FD-302a (Rev. 05-08-10)

(U//~~FOUO~~) Interview of Richard Gates 04/11/2018

Continuation of FD-302 of _____ , On 04/11/2018 , Page 6 of 6

b6
b7A
b7B per DOJ/OIP
b7C

04/11/2018
b6
b7A
b7B per DOJ/OIP
b7C

2ⁿᵈ statement

1ˢᵗ statement

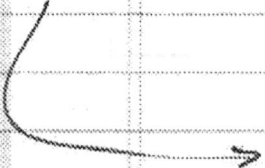

b6
b7A
b7B per DOJ/OIP
b7C

HH, RG, PM   discussion of poss

Nobody on campaign took action on

b6
b7C

Kyrgyzstan realtor group

Campaign personnel thought

Planning a press strategy, comms campaign, messaging based on emails   b6
b7A
b7B per DOJ/OIP
b7C

• Conversations, what can we plan for in way of emails

- PM/RG focused on mitigating hit pieces on PM

Eno July- 8/9

b6
b7A
b7B per DOJ/OIP
b7C

Late July – 6/19

[redacted box]

[redacted box]

[redacted box]

· Camp trying to work w/ RNC opps res team

· Didn't focus on Super PAC contrib, more camp contrib

· [redacted box]

· [redacted box] was aware of foreign contrib to HRC camp

b6
b7A
b7B per DOJ/OIP
b7C

July 22

· Campaign very happy about release

· DJT is advised to not react to releases, let it play out

[redacted box] PM, excitement [redacted box]

b6
b7A
b7B per DOJ/OIP
b7C

[redacted box] said there would be additional information

June 12 – July 22

· [redacted box]

· PM [redacted box] when release

· RG [redacted box] when release

· DJT was frustrated releases weren't happening

b6
b7A
b7B per DOJ/OIP
b7C

[redacted box]

[redacted box]

[redacted box]

[redacted box]

④

June 12 - July 22

[redacted]
b6
b7A
b7B per DOJ/OIP
b7C

[redacted]

- messaging strategy being built around poss release/content

[redacted]

- disagreement on where info came from or camp

· Does not recall PM asking KK to reach out to Russia contacts
· PM did not ask RG to call KK

[redacted]
b6
b7A
b7B per DOJ/OIP
b7C

[redacted]

· How to clean up fall out w/ Deripaska, clean up image in media
    - position PM to work w/ pro West group in Ukraine

· Financial damages
· Bad PR, Ponzles, relationship w/ Deripaska

[redacted]
b6
b7C

July 22

· PM [redacted]
b6
b7A
b7B per DOJ/OIP
b7C

· does not recall [redacted] saying [redacted] would come out

(5)

July 22

• Pivot to 'how do we use released info' → [REDACTED]

• RG doesn't believe [REDACTED]

[REDACTED] (post 7/22)

• Comment by DJT on 7/27 was ad lib "Russia if you're listening"

• No conversation [REDACTED] post 7/22 about additional information available

(post 7/22) • RG/PM spoke about obtaining missing emails, PM to talk about obtaining [REDACTED]

• Staff meeting convo about 'someone out there has to have missing emails'

• [REDACTED]

August 2

[REDACTED]

[REDACTED]

Aug 2 - Aug 21

• [REDACTED]

[REDACTED]

[REDACTED]

• [REDACTED]

• [REDACTED]

• [REDACTED]

(6)

[REDACTED BOX]

· Focus still on missing emails

· RG said no one used landlines bc there were no walls

    - everyone used cell phones

Oct 4

[REDACTED BOX]

Sept

· RG [REDACTED]

[REDACTED BOX]

· [REDACTED] upcoming info narrative

· RG was limited in Sept, work becomes w/ digital folks

Oct 7

· EG not aware of convos re: timing of release 45 mins after AH tape

[REDACTED BOX]

· [REDACTED BOX]

Oct 2016

· RNC was looking through releases

· Camp would pull press releases together [and] on RNC res and media res

· Still pursuit of ____ missing emails by camp

[redacted]   b6
                      b7C

[redacted]   b6
                      b7A
                      b7B per DOJ/OIP
                      b7C

· Caputo

[redacted] "   "   b6
                                    b7A
                                    b7B per DOJ/OIP
[redacted]   b7C

[redacted]   b6
                      b7A
                      b7B per DOJ/OIP
                      b7C

6/20 Caputo fired

   - Projects related to Caputo's camp work   b6
   - Post 6/20, other side projects [redacted]   b7A
                                                              b7B per DOJ/OIP
                                                              b7C

FD-302 (Rev. 5-8-10)

b7E
b7A

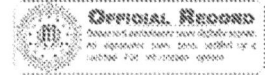

UNCLASSIFIED//FOUO

FEDERAL BUREAU OF INVESTIGATION

Date of entry   11/09/2018

Richard William Gates III was interviewed at the offices of Sidley Austin LLP located at 1501 K Street, N.W., Washington, D.C., 20005. Present for the interview were Senior Special Counsel Attorneys (SASC) Andrew Weissmann and Jeannie Rhee, Assistant Special Counsel (ASC) Aaron Zelinsky, and Special Agents [   ]. Gates's attorney, Tom Green of Sidley Austin LLP, was also present. After being advised of the identity of the interviewers and the nature of the interview, Gates provided the following information:

b6
b7C

June 12, 2016 to July 22, 2016

[Agent Note: According to open sources, on 06/12/2016, Julian Assange (Assange) said during an interview on British television channel ITV that "we have upcoming leaks in relation to Hillary Clinton... we have emails pending publication, that is correct." Assange did not specify when or how many emails would be published.]

b6
b7A
b7B per DOJ/OIP
b7C

Trump was generally frustrated Clinton's missing emails had not been found.

UNCLASSIFIED//FOUO

Investigation on   10/25/2018   at   Washington, District Of Columbia, United States (In Person)

File # [   ]   Date drafted   10/25/2018

by [   ]

b6
b7C
b7E
b7A

This document contains neither recommendations nor conclusions of the FBI. It is the property of the FBI and is loaned to your agency; it and its contents are not to be distributed outside your agency.

FBI(19cv1278)-32

UNCLASSIFIED//~~FOUO~~

Manafort was having Gates periodically call [   ] to check in on where the information was and when it would be coming.

Gates recalled a conversation with [   ] prior to 07/22 [   ] told Gates WikiLeaks would be dropping information [   ]

b6
b7A
b7B per DOJ/OIP
b7C

[   ] Gates said the Russia theory was in contradiction to the "inside job" theory that was floated later.

Gates said a messaging strategy was being built in the June/July 2016 timeframe surrounding the upcoming release of information. [   ] [   ] was building this strategy with Manafort also involved. [   ]

b6
b7A
b7B per DOJ/OIP
b7C

[   ] Clinton's trustworthiness at this time was low.

Post July 22, 2016 WikiLeaks Releases

Gates said the campaign was very happy about the WikiLeaks Democratic National Committee (DNC) releases on 07/22/2016. [   ]

b6
b7A
b7B per DOJ/OIP
b7C

Manafort, [   ] were happy from a communications team perspective because it offered a mode of deflection for the campaign after a sink in polling numbers following Trump's comments about Ted Cruz's

FD-302a (Rev. 05-08-10)

UNCLASSIFIED//~~FOUO~~

(U//FOUO) Interview of Richard Gates 10/25
Continuation of FD-302 of /2018 - _____ , On 10/25/2018 , Page 3 of 8

father at the end of the Republican National Convention (RNC) [Agent Note:
The 2016 Republican National Convention took place in Cleveland, Ohio from
07/18/2016 - 07/21/2016].

Gates said that at the time of the 07/22/2016 WikiLeaks releases, there
were public indications that Russia was behind them.

FD-302a (Rev. 05-08-10)

UNCLASSIFIED/~~FOUO~~

b6
b7A
b7B per DOJ/OIP
b7C
b7E

(U//FOUO) Interview of Richard Gates 10/25

Continuation of FD-302 of /2018 -   , On 10/25/2018 , Page   4 of 8

b6
b7A
b7B per DOJ/OIP
b7C

Gates said that after the Democratic National Convention in late July 2016 [Agent Note: The 2016 Democratic National Convention was held in Philadelphia, Pennsylvania from 07/25/2016 - 07/28/2016] or in early August 2016,

b6
b7A
b7B per DOJ/OIP
b7C

Trump and Gates were in a car transiting from Trump Tower to LaGuardia Airport (LGA).

b6
b7A
b7B per DOJ/OIP
b7C

Gates gathered that during this phone call there would be additional leaks coming. Gates thought this because shortly after boarding the plane Trump stated that more leaks were coming.

Manafort was getting pressure regarding   information, Manafort instructed Gates   status updates on upcoming information.

b6
b7A
b7B per DOJ/OIP
b7C

FD-302a (Rev. 05-08-10)

UNCLASSIFIED//FOUO

b6
b7A
b7B per DOJ/OIP
b7C
b7E

(U//FOUO) Interview of Richard Gates 10/25

Continuation of FD-302 of /2018 - , On 10/25/2018 , Page 5 of 8

b6
b7A
b7B per DOJ/OIP
b7C

Gates said around this time Kellyanne Conway (Conway) and Stephen Bannon (Bannon) were appointed to the campaign and there were conversations behind the scenes about bringing people on to bolster Manafort.

Gates said there was a strategy to defend Manafort by attacking Podesta. The idea was that Podesta had baggage as well. Gates said it was unfortunate the information did not come out in time to defend Manafort from his ultimate departure from the campaign [Agent Note: On 08/19/2016, Manafort resigned from the campaign].

October 4, 2016

b6
b7A
b7B per DOJ/OIP
b7C

October 7, 2016

Gates said that on 10/07/2016 he was not in New York and was likely in Richmond, VA or Washington, D.C. Gates's primary contacts on the campaign at this time were [   ] and Brad Parscale (Parscale).

b6
b7C

Gates advised he wasn't given a heads up on the Access Hollywood tape (the tape), but subsequently talked to members of the campaign, specifically Parscale, about it. Gates recalled the Parscale conversation being retrospective occurring on or about 10/08/2016. Parscale had told Gates he was in the room when the tape was outed. Parscale described this as a difficult time. Gates said a reporter had reached out to [   ] to give a heads up that the tape would be made public. Gates said there was a

FD-302a (Rev. 05-08-10)

UNCLASSIFIED//~~FOUO~~

very short period of time between the heads up and when the story broke.

b6
b7A
b7B per DOJ/OIP
b7C

Gates said there was no prior discussion about the tape before the heads up to the campaign.

b6
b7A
b7B per DOJ/OIP
b7C

b6
b7A
b7B per DOJ/OIP
b7C

UNCLASSIFIED//~~FOUO~~

FBI(19cv1278)-37

FD-302a (Rev. 05-08-10)

b6
b7A
b7B per DOJ/OIP
b7C
b7E

UNCLASSIFIED//FOUO

(U//FOUO) Interview of Richard Gates 10/25

Continuation of FD-302 of /2018 - _____ , On 10/25/2018 , Page 7 of 8

b6
b7A
b7B per DOJ/OIP
b7C

Gates recalls discussions about content of the Podesta emails after their release. Gates said there were discussions about how many WikiLeaks would drop each day of the 30,000 they had.

b6
b7A
b7B per DOJ/OIP
b7C

b6
b7A
b7B per DOJ/OIP
b7C
b7E

UNCLASSIFIED//~~FOUO~~

b6
b7A
b7B per DOJ/OIP
b7C

** Gates was shown an email [   ]
containing the subject line "Trump adviser: Wikileaks plotting email dump
to derail Hillary" **

Gates did not recall receiving the aforementioned email.

** Gates was shown an email [   ]
containing the subject line "Russia? Look who's really in bed with Moscow
-- Podesta & Clinton Foundation money-laundering with Russia" **

b6
b7A
b7B per DOJ/OIP
b7C

AW, ▢ JR, AZ, ▢   10/25/18   b6
RG., ▢   b7C

_10/7_   RG not in NY, Richmond or DC
        Primary contacts ▢ Brad Parscal
        No heads up the tape, subsequently talked to campaign about it
        Talked to BP
                                  —Retrospective
                                     10/8 convo
        BP in room w/ DJT when taped released, difficult time
        Reporter had reached out to ▢ given heads up
        Very small heads up before story broke   b6
        ▢   b7A
                                                       b7B per DOJ/OIP
        ▢   b7C

        No prior discussion about tape, ▢
        Talked to BP on 10/8 about tape
        ▢   b6
                                                       b7A
        ▢   b7B per DOJ/OIP
                                                       b7C

        ▢
        ▢

        ▢
        ▢
                                                       b6
        ▢   b7A
                                                       b7B per DOJ/OIP
                                                       b7C
        ▢
        ▢

FBI(19cv1278)-40

[REDACTED]

b6
b7A
b7B per DOJ/OIP
b7C

[REDACTED]

[REDACTED]

Discussion about content of emails after the fact

Discussion about how much they would drop each day about ~ of the 30,000 [illegible]

July 22

Casey was very happy about WL release

[REDACTED]

b6
b7A
b7B per DOJ/OIP
b7C

Just finished convention

[REDACTED]

[REDACTED]

RJM & [REDACTED] was happy from a comms perspective, offered [illegible] for camp

after sink in polls at last moment & conv. DJT comments about
Ted Cruz's father

[REDACTED]

b6
b7A
b7B per DOJ/OIP
b7C

Public indications Russia was behind it

[redacted]

~ In contradiction to inside job theory floated at the time later

[redacted]

[redacted]

b6
b7A
b7B per DOJ/OIP
b7C

[redacted]

[redacted]

August 2

TT → LCA,

⑦

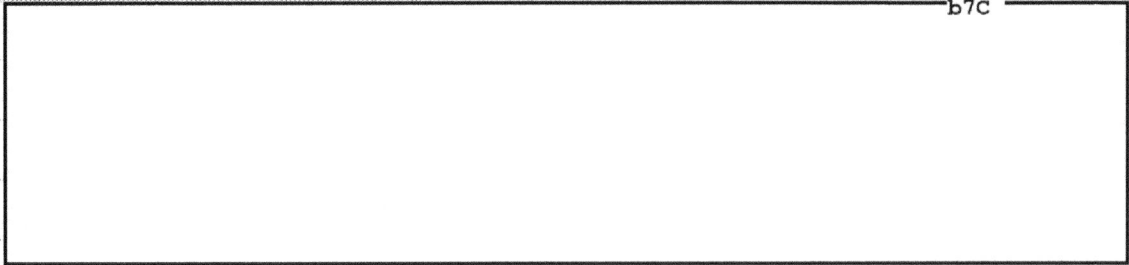

[box - redacted]

Strategy to defend PJM, by attacking Edwards
idea was Edwards had baggage as well

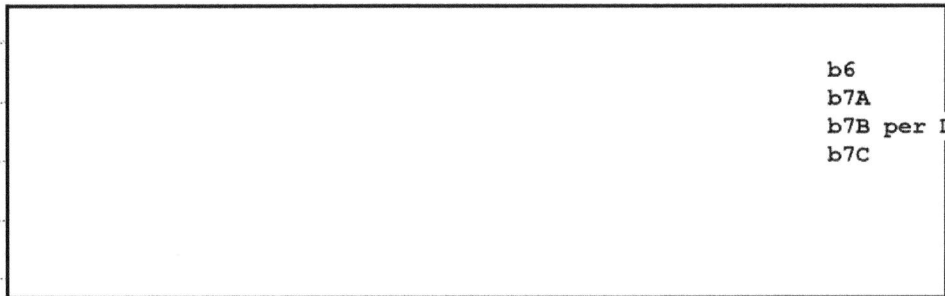

[box - redacted]

KC & SB had been expanded, canvas listed the
scenes about bringing people on to bolster PJM

[box - redacted]

FBI(19cv1278)-46

10/4

[redacted]

6/12   JA announcement, pending natural rel HPC, pending publication

[redacted]

[redacted]

PK furnished the missing emails had not been found.

[redacted]

Managing Strategy, from July, surrounding ongoing release of info

[redacted] building strategy, PM involved

```
                                                                    b6
                                                                    b7A
                                                                    b7B per DOJ/OIP
                                                                    b7C
```

* RG reads article from [ ] email *

```
                                                                    b6
                                                                    b7A
                                                                    b7B per DOJ/OIP
                                                                    b7C
```

* RG down email from 10/7 *

```
                                                                    b6
                                                                    b7A
                                                                    b7B per DOJ/OIP
                                                                    b7C
```

From:
Sent:
To:
cc:
Subject: Trump adviser: Wikileaks plotting email dump to derail hillary

b6
b7A
b7B per DOJ/OIP
b7C

http://www.wnd.com/2016/08/trump-adviser-wikileaks-plotting-email-dump-to-derail-hillary/

TRUMP ADVISER: WIKILEAKS PLOTTING EMAIL DUMP TO DERAIL HILLARY

Hillary Clinton (Photo: Twitter)

NEW YORK – A top Trump adviser says his computer and personal bank accounts were hacked in retaliation for declaring publicly he believes Julian Assange of WikiLeaks has a complete set of Hillary Clinton's 30,000 scrubbed "private emails" and is preparing to release them to derail the Democratic Party nominee's presidential campaign.

Roger Stone, co-author of the bestselling book "The Clintons' War on Women" and a longtime friend of Trump, told WND in an interview that he has communicated directly with Assange.

"In the next series of emails Assange plans to release, I have reason to believe the Clinton Foundation scandals will surface to keep Bill and Hillary from returning to the White House," he said.

The Clintons' scheme to monetize the White House for personal profit is exposed in "Partners in Crime." Order it now at the WND Superstore!

Stone notes Assange's release of DNC-hacked emails just before the start of the party's Philadelphia presidential nominating convention caused Debbie Wasserman Schultz to resign as DNC chairman for her favoring Clinton over challenger Bernie Sanders.

The next batch, Stone said, include Clinton's communications with State Department aides Cheryl Mills and Huma Abedin.

ELECTION 2016

TRUMP ADVISER: WIKILEAKS PLOTTING EMAIL DUMP TO DERAIL HILLARY

Claims he was hacked after disclosing what Assange told him

Published: 08/15/2016 at 7:36 PM

JEROME R. CORSI (HTTPS://WWW.WND.COM/AUTHOR/JCORSI/) About | Email
(mailto:jcorsi@worldnetdaily.com) | Archive (https://www.wnd.com/author/jcorsi/?
archive=true)

Subscribe to feed (https://www.wnd.com/author/jcorsi/feed/)

(/files/2016/08/Hillary-Clinton-TW3.jpg)
Hillary Clinton (Photo: Twitter)

(https://www.wnd.com/;

NEW YORK – A top Trump adviser says his computer and personal bank accounts were hacked in retaliation for declaring publicly he believes Julian Assange of Wikileaks has a complete set of Hillary Clinton's 30,000 scrubbed "private emails" and is preparing to release them to derail the Democratic Party nominee's presidential campaign.

Roger Stone, co-author of the bestselling book "The Clintons' War on Women" and a longtime friend of Trump, told WND in an interview that he has communicated directly with Assange.

"In the next series of emails Assange plans to release I have reason to believe the Clinton Foundation scandals will surface to keep Bill and Hillary from returning to the White House," he said.

The Clintons' scheme to monetize the White House for personal profit is exposed in "Partners in Crime." Order it now at the WND Superstore! (http://superstore.wnd.com/Partners-in-Crime-Hardcover-Jerome-Corsi)

Stone noted Assange's release of DNC-hacked emails just before the start of the party's Philadelphia presidential nominating convention caused Debbie Wasserman Schultz to resign as DNC chairman for her favoring Clinton over challenger Bernie Sanders.

The next batch, Stone said, include Clinton's communications with State Department aides Cheryl Mills and Huma Abedin.

He said the hackers who penetrated his personal bank accounts managed to establish an online portal through which they began stealing money before they were detected and stopped.

"Major portions of the hard drive on my computer system were destroyed, erasing maybe permanently decades of email contacts and various writing projects that were yet in progress," he said.

Stone told WND that while he has hired a team of computer experts to determine if his lost computer files can be recovered, he believes much of the damage is permanent, forcing him to move into a more highly secured computer environment.

In a speech Southwest Broward Republican Organization in Florida, published Aug. 9 by David Brock's left-wing website Media Matters (https://mediamatters.org/video/2016/08/09/roger-stone-confirms-hes-communication-julian-assange/212261), Stone said he had "communicated with Assange."

"I believe the next tranche of his documents pertain to the Clinton Foundation, but there is no telling what the October surprise may be," he said.

Stone told WND that Assange "plans to drop at various strategic points in the presidential campaigns Hillary Clinton emails involving the Clinton Foundation that have yet to surface publically."

"Assange claims the emails contain enough damaging information to put Hillary Clinton in jail for selling State Department 'official acts' in exchange for contributions to the Clinton Foundation and as a reward for Clinton Foundation donors becoming clients of Teneo, the consulting firm established by Bill Clinton's White House 'body man' Doug Band," he said.

"The Democrats are right to fear Assange's next email drops will be devastating to Hillary."

Stone, in an Info Wars interview last Friday with Alex Jones (https://www.youtube.com/watch?v=VQKHmvgMtFc), first disclosed his computer and bank accounts had been hacked.

Clinton Foundation conflicts of interest

In May 2013, Politico broke the story (http://www.politico.com/story/2013/05/huma-abedin-consultant-state-091503) that longtime Hillary Clinton aide Huma Abedin spent her final months at the State Department working as a "special government employee" in a part-time consultancy, beginning during her pregnancy in the summer of 2012, while she worked second job as a part-time consultant to Teneo.

The New York Post in September 2013 (https://nypost.com/2013/09/25/state-dept-sued-over-huma-abedin-pay-deal/) reported Abedin was being paid $355,000 as a consultant to Teneo while receiving $135,000 in government pay as a part-time consultant for Hillary Clinton.

The Washington Post revealed in an article published Aug. 27, 2015, (https://www.washingtonpost.com/politics/how-huma-abedin-operated-at-the-center-of-the-clinton-universe/2015/08/27/cd099eee-4b32-11e5-902f-39e9219e574b_story.html) that Abedin actually held four different jobs simultaneously, being paid also by the Clinton Foundation, where she was a contractor preparing for Hillary Clinton's eventual transition from the State Department to the charity.

Last Thursday, CNN reported (https://www.cnn.com/2016/08/11/politics/hillary-clinton-cgi-cheryl-mills/) Mills, on June 19, 2012, while serving as chief of staff for Secretary of State Clinton, traveled to New York to interview candidates for top jobs in the Clinton Foundation.

'The tangled web'

Drivers with No Tickets in 3 Years Should Do This in 2018

Everquote
(//trends.revcontent.com/click.php?
d=Fkd%2BagQ2yvfYpjmLCjA4EUyoA4agOnGo%2BjLPlsl9E4Jz7yZMvMN81vpob8CUU(
X

Find Out More >   ⚡ 86,546

Last September, Citizens United published three Freedom of Information Act email releases (http://www.citizensunited.org/press-releases.aspx?article=10113) that yielded dozens of Hillary Clinton emails that documented Mills and Abedin had been in regular contact with both the Clinton Foundation and with Doug Band via his email at his consulting firm, Teneo.

The decision by Citizens United to publish the emails in their entirety triggered a firestorm of criticism in the media. David Bossie, founder of Citizens United, said the emails show the "tangled web that is the State Department, Teneo, and the Clinton Foundation." (https://www.washingtonpost.com/politics/how-huma-abedin-operated-at-the-center-of-the-clinton-universe/2015/08/27/cd099eee-4b32-11e5-902f-39e9219e574b_story.html)

"The Clinton Foundation had a direct line to Hillary Clinton's former chief of staff at the State Department, seeking her advice on lucrative speaking invitations for former President Bill Clinton outside of the department's normal ethics process, according to emails that surfaced in a federal lawsuit," reporter Rachael Bade wrote in Politico on Sept. 30, 2015, in an article titled "Clinton's chief of staff gave advice to Clinton Foundation."

"Foundation officials sought guidance from Cheryl Mills, a longtime Clinton lawyer and friend, on whether the former president should accept paid speaking gigs in countries that could have presented public relations problems, including a North Korea appearance that the nonprofit said Hillary Clinton's brother was pushing, the emails show," Bade continued.

Noting that Mills sat on the Clinton Foundation board before becoming the State Department's No. 2 employee, Bade commented that "Mills' involvement with some of the most sensitive speaking requests shows that top foundation officials felt comfortable seeking advice directly from Hillary Clinton's closest adviser and consulted her privately on speaking requests involving hundreds of thousands of dollars."

Bade also reported that the attorney for Mills, Beth Wilkinson, a partner at Paul, Weiss, Rifkind, Wharton & Garrison LLP, argued that her client simply gave advice and did not officially approve the arrangements, insisting no State Department rules had been broken.

"A member of Hillary Clinton's staff at the Department of State emailed classified information about the government in Congo to a staffer at the Clinton Foundation in 2012," wrote Alana Goodman in a September 2015 Washington Free Beacon article commenting on one of the emails Citizens United published. (http://freebeacon.com/politics/clinton-aide-shared-classified-information-with-foundation-email-shows/)

Goodman reported Mills sent the email to the Clinton Foundation foreign policy director, Amitabh Desai, on July 12, 2012, commenting that the FOIA-released email had been partially redacted because it included "foreign government information" that has been classified as "Confidential" by the State Department.

"The message could add to concerns from congressional and FBI investigators about whether former Secretary Clinton and her aides mishandled classified information while at the State Department," Goodman reported. "The email, which discussed the relationship between the governments in Rwanda and the Democratic Republic of Congo, was originally drafted by Johnnie Carson, the State Department's assistant secretary for African affairs, who sent it to Mills' State Department email address."

Goodman further reported that Mills later forwarded the full message to Desai along with "talking points" for former President Bill Clinton shortly before he was scheduled to visit the region.

Popular in the Community

'TRANSGENDER' IS A POLITICAL TEST, NOT...

AnitaHaircut
3d

The goats on the left will never be satisfie...

FREEDOM FROM RELIGION FOUNDATIO...

Melissa Sederoff
9h

The FFRF as well as other liberal...

(https://dynamic-cdn.spot.im/yad/optout.html)

Note: Read our discussion guidelines (/discussion-guidelines/) before commenting.

TRIAL (HTTP://SUPERSTORE.WND.COM/WND-WEEKLY-FREE-SAMPLE) / MONTHLY (HTTP://SUPERSTORE.WND.COM/WND-WEEKLY-MONTH-TO-MONTH) / ANNUAL (HTTP://SUPERSTORE.WND.COM/WND-WEEKLY-1-YEAR-SUBSCRIPTION)

SUBSCRIBE (HTTP://SUPERSTORE.WND.COM/WHISTLEBLOWER-MAGAZINE) / GIFT (HTTP://SUPERSTORE.WND.COM/WHISTLEBLOWER-MAGAZINE-GIFT) / RENEW (HTTP://SUPERSTORE.WND.COM/WHISTLEBLOWER-MAGAZINE-RENEWAL)

From:	b6
Sent:	b7A
To:	b7B per DOJ/OIP
CC:	b7C

Subject: Russia? Look who's really in bed with Moscow – Podesta & Clinton Foundation money-laundering with Russia

http://www.wnd.com/2016/10/hillary-campaign-chief-tied-to-russian-money-laundering/

Russia? Look who's really in bed with Moscow

Hillary campaign chief, Clinton Foundation, in deep on international money-laundering

Published: 15 hours ago

ELECTION 2016

ELECTION 2016

RUSSIA? LOOK WHO'S REALLY IN BED WITH MOSCOW

Hillary campaign chief, Clinton Foundation, in deep on international money-laundering

Published: 10/06/2016 at 8:27 PM

JEROME R. CORSI (HTTPS://WWW.WND.COM/AUTHOR/JCORSI/)   About | Email (mailto:jcorsi@worldnetdaily.com) | Archive (https://www.wnd.com/author/jcorsi/?archive=true)

🔖 Subscribe to feed (https://www.wnd.com/author/jcorsi/feed/)

(/files/2013/12/podesta.jpg)
John Podesta

(https://www.wnd.com/?

🖶 Print

NEW YORK – Hillary Clinton's presidential campaign manager, John Podesta, was on the executive board of a client of the Panamanian law firm Mossack Fonseca, which is at the heart of the the Panama Papers (https://panamapapers.icij.org/) investigation into massive global offshore money-laundering.

The company for which Podesta served as a board member, Joule, also received $35 million from a Putin-connected Russian government fund at the same time then-Secretary of State Hillary Clinton spearheaded the transfer of U.S. advanced technology, some with military uses, as part of her "reset" strategy with Russia, according to a report titled "From Russia With Money," (http://www.g-a-i.org/u/2016/08/Report-Skolkvovo-08012016.pdf) released in August by the Government Accountability Institute (http://www.g-a-i.org/about/). "Clinton Cash" author Peter Schweizer is president of GAI, and Steve Bannon, the CEO of the Trump campaign, is a director.

The Clintons' corruption is exposed in Jerome Corsi''s "Partners in Crime: The Clintons' Scheme to Monetize the White House for Personal Profit," available at the WND Superstore! (http://superstore.wnd.com/Partners-in-Crime-Hardcover-Bulk?promocode=STORY)

The Russian entities that funneled money to Joule and its related companies, and ultimately to Podesta, include a controversial Russian investor with ties to the Russian government, Viktor Vekselberg, and his Renova Group, a Russian conglomerate with interests in oil, energy and telecommunication.

Vekselberg is a board member of Rusnano (http://search.en.rusnano.com/default.aspx?k=Renova), the Russian State Investment Fund, as well as president of the Skolkovo Foundation, named for Russia's version of Silicon Valley.

The Government Accountability Institute report noted Joule was a new company, founded in 2007, pioneering a technology based on harnessing solar energy. Podesta consulted for a foundation run by one of the investors in Joule Energy, Hansjoerg Wyss, who in turn was a major Clinton Foundation donor.

The report documented the Wyss Foundation has given from $1 million to $5 million to the Clinton Foundation. Podesta was paid $87,000 by the Wyss Foundation in 2013, according to federal tax records.

In his 2014 federal government disclosure filing, Podesta declared he divested stock options from Joule, but the disclosure does not cover the years 2011-2012.

Joule Global Stichting was established in Amsterdam on March 14, 2011.

Podesta joined the company's executive board on June 25, 2011. Joule Stichting is a foundation, but it's not strictly a foundation in the charitable sense. A foundation of this type, a Dutch Stichting, is a popular means for reducing one's tax burden, as noted on the website of the Panamanian law firm Mossack Fonseca.

Drivers with No Tickets in 3 Years Should Do This in 2018

Everquote
(//trends.revcontent.com/click.php?
d=shLFnoxaShPptmzzHqEpY2hYrIRtox06Dru4S8vQICczAGqFGkREMWrykBRosenRLp
x

Find Out More >   ♠ 44,824

The Government Accountability Institute concluded that although Podesta is listed on the corporate records, he failed to disclose his membership on the board of Joule Stichting in his federal financial disclosure forms when he joined the Obama White House as a senior adviser.

Russian government invests

Two months after Podesta joined the board, the Russian government investment fund Rusnano, the Russian Corporation of Nanotechnologies, founded by Vladimir Putin in 2007, announced it would invest up to $35 million in Joule Unlimited.

On Aug. 1, Bannon and Schweizer co-authored a Breitbart.com article titled "Report: Hillary Clinton's Campaign Manager John Podesta Sat on Board of Company that Bagged $35 million from Putin-Connected Russian Government Fund." (http://www.breitbart.com/2016-presidential-race/2016/08/01/report-hillary-clintons-campaign-mgr-john-podesta-sat-board-company-bagged-35-million-putin-connected-russian-govt-fund-2/)

"The GAI investigative report says it's unclear how much, if any, money Podesta made. The reason: Podesta was on the board of three Joule entities, but only listed two on his disclosure; the most important entity, Joule Stichting, he did not list," Bannon and Schweizer noted. "Why Podesta failed to reveal, as required by law on his federal financial disclosures, his membership on the board of this offshore company is presently unknown."

Bannon and Schweizer further reported flows of funds from Russia during the "reset" to Podesta-connected entities apparently didn't end with Joule Energy, as Podesta's far-left think tank, Center for American Progress, CAP, took in $5.25 million from the Sea Change Foundation between 2010 and 2013. The Sea Change Foundation, it turns out, ties into various entities specifically named and investigated in the Panama Papers, including Klein Ltd. and Troika Dialog Ltd.

TRENDING TODAY

Feed

by Engage.IM

Hey There!

Connect your account to surface
personalized and relevant content!

Personalize with Facebook

Continue with E-mail

Already have an account?

Terms and Conditions
(//faq.engage.im/customer/en/portal/articles/2923351-
publisher-terms-conditions)

Trending Channels on Wnd.com

Love

Be the first to read.

About
15 days

| Donald | Christianity | Education | Immigration |
| Trump | | Issues | |

E **Everquote**
   Sponsored

Look who's racist now - WND

Many years ago I discovered a dirty little secret
about left-wing ideologues in the Democratic
Party. Yes, I know these terms are largely
redundant. The few remaining Democrats who
don't fit that description are either political

This Simple Method Ends Ear Ringing (Tinnitus) - Try It

Read More

Love

Be the first to react

Look who's 'desperate' for American cash

The Palestinian Authority is "desperate" for American cash to survive, yet when the U.S. cut off funding, it reacted by threatening violence, explains a new report in Joseph Farah's G2 Bulletin. ..

Love   Engage   Share

Be the first to react   0 comments

LOAD MORE CONTENT

Popular In the Community

CHARLIE DANIELS: MAXINE'S RAVING...

Rotorblade
11h

Fun Fact ..The NAZIs of Germany, built their...

MALE TEACHER ORDERED TO OBSERVE TEEN GIRL...

STEPHEN
15h

The school psychologist, and th...

Note: Read our discussion guidelines (/discussion-guidelines/) before commenting.

FD-302 (Rev. 5-8-10)

b7E

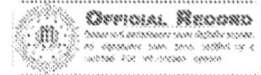

FEDERAL BUREAU OF INVESTIGATION

Date of entry   11/09/2018

(U) On 09/18/2018 Special Agents (SA) [ ] Intelligence Analyst [ ] Assistant Special Counsel L. Rush Atkinson, Senior Assistant Special Counsel (SASC) Andrew Goldstein and SASC Jeannie Rhee interviewed MICHAEL DEAN COHEN (COHEN) at his attorney's offices at 655 3rd Ave, New York, NY. Present were COHEN's legal counsel, Guy Petrillo, Amy Lester, and Philip Pilmar. Additionally, Assistant United States Attorney [ ] and SA [ ] from SDNY and FBI NY attended. In the presence of his attorney, COHEN reviewed and executed two proffer agreements, one from the Special Counsel's Office, attached, and one from SDNY, which was retained by SDNY. After being advised of the identities of the interviewing SAs and the purpose of the interview, COHEN provided the following:

b6
b7C

(U) [ ]   **b5 Per DOJ/OIP**

[ ] The TRUMP ORG wanted to terminate any deals that had to [ ]

of the Presidential Inauguration. [ ]

b5 Per DOJ/OIP

b6
b7C

(U) COHEN found [ ] TRUMP TOWER MOSCO **b5 Per DOJ/OIP** on the list. [ ]

Investigation on 09/18/2018 at New York, New York, United States (In Person)

File # [ ]   Date drafted 09/24/2018

b6
b7C
b7E

by [ ]

b5 Per DOJ/OIP

b6
b7C

b5 Per DOJ/OIP

b6
b7A
b7C

b5 Per DOJ/OIP

b5 Per DOJ/OIP

b6
b7C

b5 Per DOJ/OIP

Continuation of FD-302 of (U) Interview of Michael Cohen . On 09/18/2018 , Page 3 of 15

b5 Per DOJ/OIP

b5 Per DOJ/OIP

b6
b7C

b5 Per DOJ/OIP

(U) The use of the TRUMP ORG's "party line" with respect to Russia went earlier than the closing of TRUMP TOWER BATUMI and TRUMP TOWER MOSCOW.

b5 Per DOJ/OIP

b6
b7C

(U) COHEN spoke to TRUMP about TRUMP TOWER MOSCOW and Russia as soon as news reports started to come out. The conversations with TRUMP were earlier than the February 2017

b5 Per DOJ/OIP

b6
b7C

b5 Per DOJ/OIP

b5 Per DOJ/OIP

b5 Per DOJ/OIP

(U) TRUMP asked COHEN in March or April 2016 if anything was happening with Russia.   b5 Per DOJ/OIP

b5 Per DOJ/OIP

b5 Per DOJ/OIP

b5 Per DOJ/OIP

(U) TRUMP's July [27], 2016 statement was untrue. In July, COHEN spoke to TRUMP about the statement. TRUMP told COHEN they have no deals in Russia.

COHEN thought TRUMP justified saying this because TRUMP TOWER MOSCOW was not a deal yet. TRUMP said, "Why mention it if it is not a deal?" **b5 Per DOJ/OIP**

b5 Per DOJ/OIP

(U) MEGAN TWOHEY - *New York Times*

(U) COHEN met MEGAN TWOHEY, a new reporter at the *New York Times*, thinking it was a friendly meeting for the two to get to know each other and not a sit down interview. They met at [   ] COHE   **b6**
N recalled MEGAN TWOHEY [   ]   **b7C**

b5 Per DOJ/OIP

b6
b7C

b5 Per DOJ/OIP

COHEN told TWOHEY the project ended in January 2016 and was not feasible.

b5 Per DOJ/OIP
b7C

was part of the script TRUMP, HICKS, and KELLYANNE CONWAY (CONWAY) came up with months before. It was the party line to dismiss the notion.

b5 Per DOJ/OIP

COHEN previously talked about this script with TRUMP. COHEN did not tell TRUMP he thought the script was untrue because TRUMP already knew it was untrue.

b5 Per DOJ/OIP
b6
b7C

b5 Per DOJ/OIP

b5 Per DOJ/OIP

b5 Per DOJ/OIP
b6
b7C

b7E

b5 Per DOJ/OIP

b5 Per DOJ/OIP

b5 Per DOJ/OIP
b6
b7C

b5 Per DOJ/OIP

(U) The source for the August 2017 *Washington Post* article about TRUMP TOWER MOSCOW sounded like it came from COHEN. COHEN was holding to the script that it was abandoned in January 2016.

b5 Per DOJ/OIP

b5 Per DOJ/OIP

b5 Per DOJ/OIP

b5 Per DOJ/OIP

(U) It was not COHEN's idea to write a letter to congress about TRUMP TOWER MOSCOW. The statement was put out to piggyback off of JARED KUSHNER putting out a statement before. The release was to shape the narrative and to let other people who might be witnesses know what COHEN was saying to keep the same message. This was KUSHNER's approach to public messaging.

b5 Per DOJ/OIP

b5 Per DOJ/OIP

b5 Per DOJ/OIP

b5 Per DOJ/OIP

(U) COHEN learned the message to have the Russia investigations end early
from discussions with TRUMP, SEKULOW, [   ] The discussions occurred   b6
shortly after, in the days or weeks following, the appointment of the   b7C
Special Counsel. It would have been May or June [2017]. The discussion was
to not worry, the investigation would not last and would be over by August
-- August became December and the House and Senate investigations had not

b5 Per DOJ/OIP

b5 Per DOJ/OIP

b5 Per DOJ/OIP

b6
b7C

b5 Per DOJ/OIP

b5 Per DOJ/OIP

b5 Per DOJ/OIP

b6
b7A
(U)   b7B per DOJ/OIP
b7C

b5 Per DOJ/OIP

b5 Per DOJ/OIP

b5 Per DOJ/OIP

(U) COHEN had a second conversation with TRUMP [ ] in TRUMP's office very soon after Friday, July 22, 2016. TRUMP said to COHEN, [ ]

b5 Per DOJ/OIP

b6
b7A
b7B per DOJ/OIP
b7C

b5 Per DOJ/OIP

b5 Per DOJ/OIP

b6
b7A
b7B per DOJ/OIP
b7C

b5 Per DOJ/OIP

b5 Per DOJ/OIP

b5 Per DOJ/OIP

b5 Per DOJ/OIP

(U) In preparation for his Congressional testimony, COHEN's message had several components. COHEN had to keep TRUMP out of the messaging related to Russia and keep TRUMP out of the Russia conversation. One of these points to keep TRUMP out of was this UNGA TRUMP-Putin meeting, because he had discussed it on the HANNITY SHOW.

(U) In advance of testifying, there was a specific conversation about keeping TRUMP out of the UNGA narrative. COHEN was trying to be loyal. The investigation was not supposed to have taken us to where we are today. COHEN was told if he stayed on message, the President had his back, the President loves you.

b5 Per DOJ/OIP

b6
b7B per DOJ/OIP
b7C

b5 Per DOJ/OIP

b5 Per DOJ/OIP

b5 Per DOJ/OIP

b5 Per DOJ/OIP

b5 Per DOJ/OIP

b5 Per DOJ/OIP

b5 Per DOJ/OIP

Continuation of FD-302 of (U) Interview of Michael Cohen _____ . On 09/18/2018 . Page 13 of 15

b5 Per DOJ/OIP

b6
b7C

b5 Per DOJ/OIP

b5 Per DOJ/OIP

b5 Per DOJ/OIP

b5 Per DOJ/OIP
b7A
b7B per DOJ/OIP
b7C

b7E

b5 Per DOJ/OIP
b7A
b7B per DOJ/OIP
b7C

b5 Per DOJ/OIP

b6
b7A
b7B per DOJ/OIP
b7C

Continuation of FD-302 of (U) Interview of Michael Cohen . On 09/18/2018 , Page 15 of 15

b5 Per DOJ/OIP

b6
b7A
b7B per DOJ/OIP
b7C

Andrew Goldstein   9/18/2018
Rush Atkinson   Guy Petrillo
Jeannie Rhee   Amy Lester
   Phil Jhum
                           Michael Cohen

b6
b7C

Proffer - SCO - Intnled w/ Guy
        - SDNY - Intnled w/ Guy

b5 Per DOJ/OIP

MC -

Guy-

b6
b7C

Trump Tower "Moscow -

APL — Tracin Porter low back

APL — Russia + TTUS — when speaking to PUT
ME as early as newspaports were coming
out. — forgot when earliest article was

APL — 1st Article — Febr. 2017 —

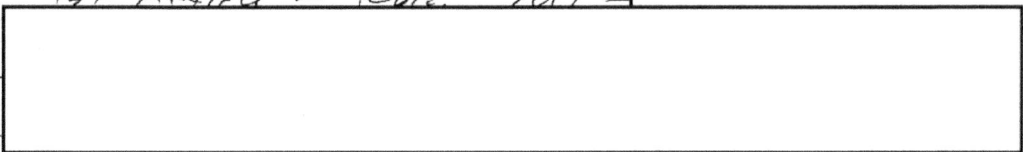

APL

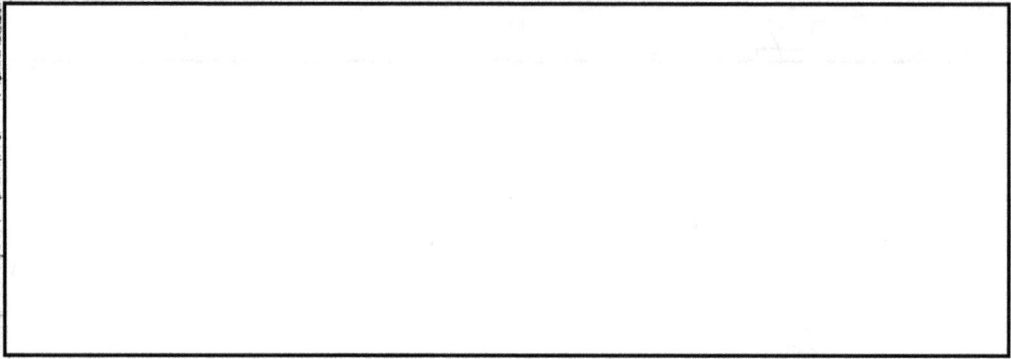
b5 Per DOJ/OIP

b6
b7C

b5 Per DOJ/OIP

ADD

b6
b7C

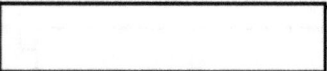

— ask n March o April

anytime happening w/ Russia —

b5 Per DOJ/OIP

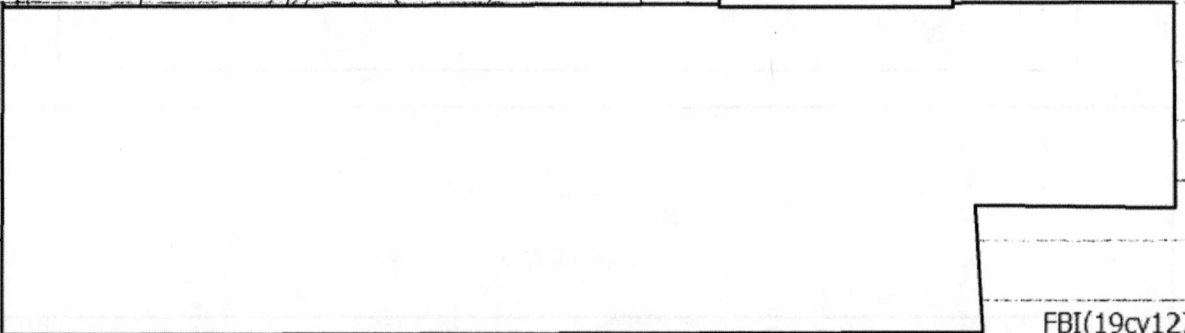

APC

FBI(19cv1278)-83

NC ─

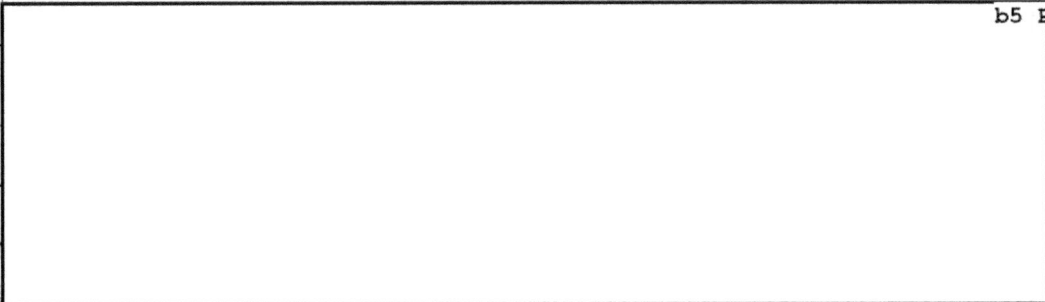

APB DJT's statement in July — MC not true

MC — spoke to DJT abt statement and

in relation to roscoe — DJT we have no clue

if it happens — when it happens — why

mention it — it is not actual

APG — Russia Theme

Theory

b5 Per DOJ/OIP

ADG
read
reports

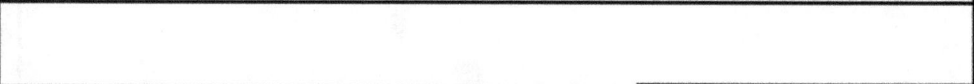

b5 Per DOJ/OIP

w/a end at Jones —

ADG

MC

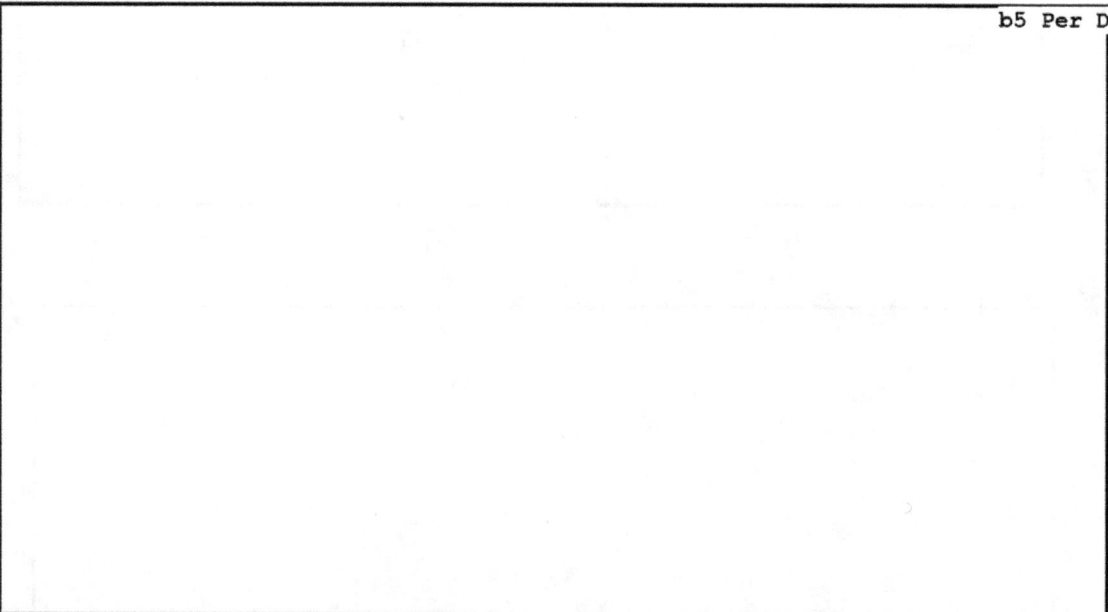

b5 Per DOJ/OIP

b6
b7C

↔ DJT, Hope, Comey

this is the _____ line - Decide
motion -

AB

- 1/4/___ about this script w/ DJT
APB script is fake - talk/w/ DJT about _____
V__ DO - he already knew it.

APB

b5 Per DOJ/OIP

APC—

ADM—

f.w   b6
                                             b7C

APG— 8/27 +28 — newstorys start 11/17

b5 Per DOJ/OIP

APG—WaPost says absolutely by Jan
   —me sounds like would come from me

b5 Per DOJ/OIP

Script — absolute Jan 2016 —

APG—

b5 Per DOJ/OIP

JSR — [b5 Per DOJ/OIP]

JSR — [b5 Per DOJ/OIP]

MC — [b5 Per DOJ/OIP]

JSR — [b5 Per DOJ/OIP]

APor — yes or No Q
  Idea to write letter to Congress about
  TTor ?
  MC — NO

[b5 Per DOJ/OIP]

Guy — Statement got out — Piggyback off of Jared Kushner's letter to Chair
JSP — even if worded — your idea ?
MC — not [no], not his idea —

JSR [b5 Per DOJ/OIP]

MC — Shape narrative, let other people
  who might be witnesses to let them
  know what he was saying — keep
  narrative + shape message.

JSR—JK approach to Public messg?
    nc — yes, Ma'am

b5 Per DOJ/OIP

b5 Per DOJ/OIP

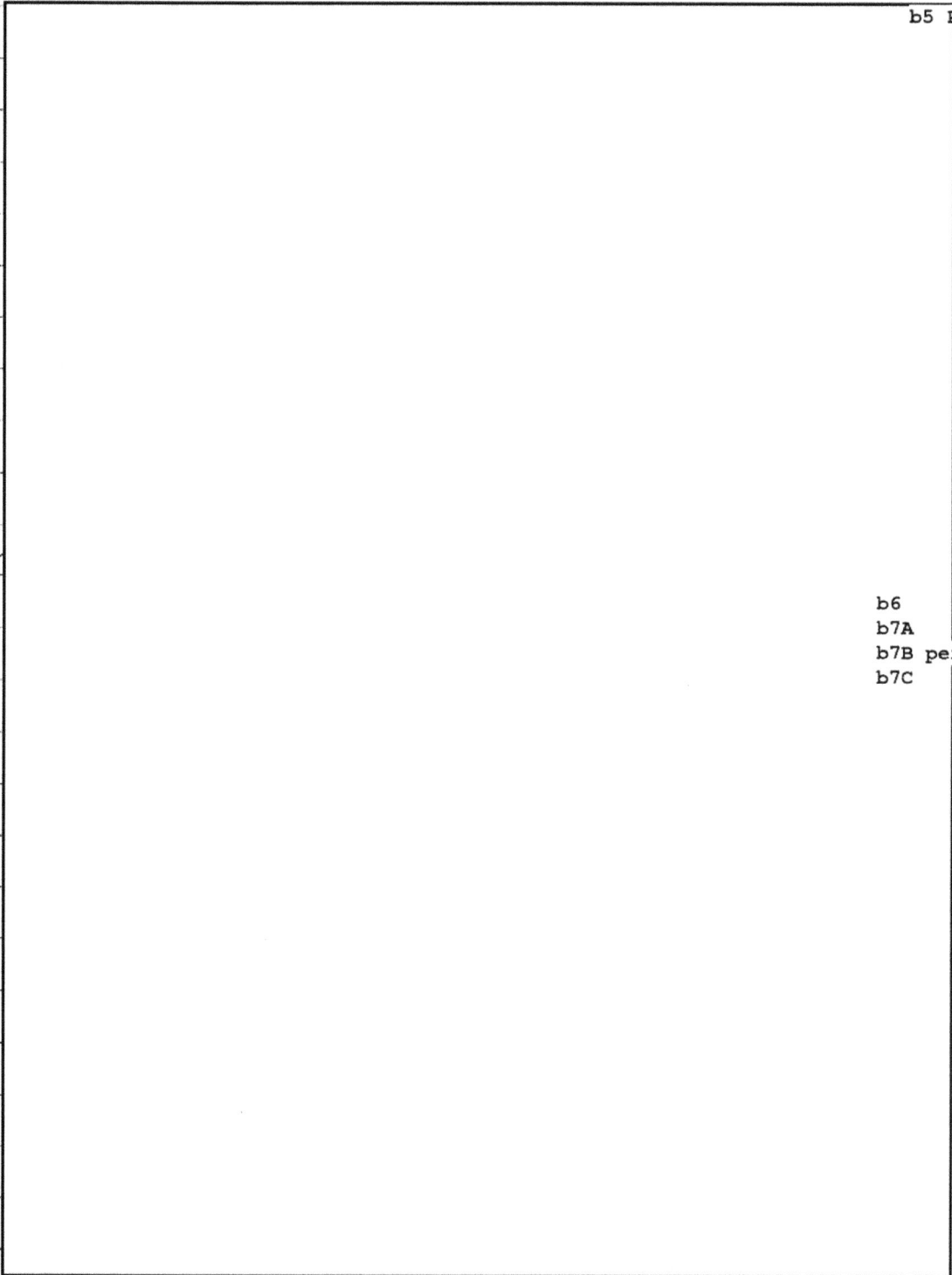

b5 Per DOJ/OIP

b6
b7A
b7B per DOJ/OIP
b7C

M

Trl contto afte release

22nd - Friday - afte to 22nd

AJT said

b5 Per DOJ/OIP

LPA

ADG

APA — boy 17th congressional testimony — (orians?)
MC — message had several corporate
keep trump out of message, Russia
keep out of Russia issue.
Decided — talking points was Trump Putin
meeting — Re Hmm…
APA — in advance of testify is dangerous.
Specific issues about keep trump out
of this episode, try to be loyal.
Investigate has not supposed to take
us to where we are today.
Stay on message — Russ has been seek. Pres

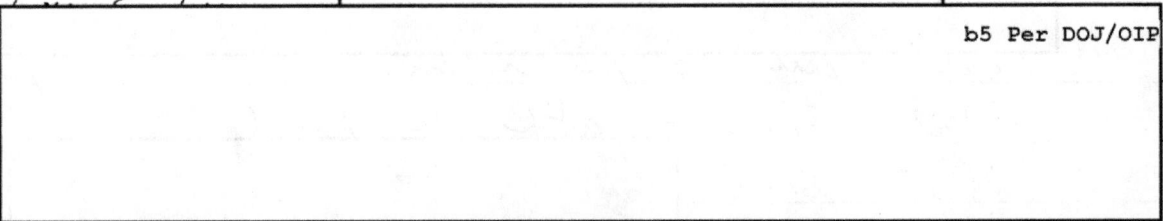

U.S. Department of Justice
The Special Counsel's Office

Washington, D.C. 20530

August 6, 2018

Guy Petrillo
Petrillo Klein & Boxer LLP
655 Third Ave.
22nd Floor
New York, NY 10017

      Re: Michael D. Cohen

Dear Counsel:

You have indicated that your client Michael D. Cohen (hereinafter "Client"), is interested in providing information to the government.

With respect to the meeting between the government, Client and yourself on August 7, 2018 (hereinafter "the meeting"), the government will be represented by individuals from the Special Counsel's Office and the Federal Bureau of Investigation. The terms of this letter do not bind any office or component of the U.S. Department of Justice other than those identified in the preceding sentence. The following terms and conditions apply to the meeting:

(1)   **THIS IS NOT A COOPERATION AGREEMENT.** Client has agreed to provide information to the government, and to respond to questions truthfully and completely. By receiving Client's proffer, the government does not agree to make any motion on Client's behalf or to enter into a cooperation agreement, plea agreement, immunity agreement or non- prosecution agreement with Client. The government makes no representation about the likelihood that any such agreement will be reached in connection with this meeting.

(2)   Should Client be prosecuted, no statements made by Client during the meeting will be used against Client in the government's case-in-chief at trial or for purposes of sentencing, except as provided below.

(3)   The government may use any statement made or information provided by Client, or on Client's behalf, in a prosecution for false statements, perjury, or obstruction of justice, premised on statements or actions during the meeting. The government may also use any such statement or information at sentencing in support of an argument that Client failed to provide truthful or complete information during the meeting, and, accordingly: (a) that under the United States Sentencing Guidelines, Client is not entitled to a downward adjustment for acceptance of

responsibility pursuant to Section 3E1.1, or should receive an upward adjustment for obstruction of justice pursuant to Section 3C1.1; and (b) that Client's conduct at the meeting is a relevant factor under 18 U.S.C. § 3553(a).

(4)   The government may make derivative use of any statements made or other information provided by Client during the meeting. Therefore, the government may pursue any investigative leads obtained directly or indirectly from such statements and information and may use the evidence or information subsequently obtained therefrom against Client in any manner and in any proceeding.

(5)   In any proceeding, including sentencing, the government may use Client's statements and any information provided by Client during or in connection with the meeting to cross-examine Client, to rebut any evidence or arguments offered on Client's behalf, or to address any issues or questions raised by a court on its own initiative.

(6)   Neither this agreement nor the meeting constitutes a plea discussion or an attempt to initiate plea discussions. In the event this agreement or the meeting is later construed to constitute a plea discussion or an attempt to initiate plea discussions, Client knowingly and voluntarily waives any right Client might have under Fed. R. Evid. 410, Fed. R. Crim. P. 11(f), or otherwise, to prohibit the use against Client of statements made or information provided during the meeting.

(7)   The government reserves the right to argue that neither this agreement nor the meeting constitutes the timely provision of complete information to the government concerning Client's involvement in an offense, within the meaning of Section 3E1.1(b) of the Sentencing Guidelines.

(8)   If and when required to do so by a court, the government may disclose to the Probation Office or the court any statements and information provided by Client during the meeting.

(9)   The government may disclose the fact of the meeting or the information provided by Client during the meeting to the extent the government determines in its sole discretion that disclosure would be in furtherance of its discharge of its duties and responsibilities or is otherwise required by law. Such disclosure includes disclosure to a local, state, federal, or foreign government office or agency, including but not limited to another prosecutor's office, if the recipient of the information agrees to abide by the relevant terms of this agreement.

(10)   The terms and conditions set forth in this agreement extend, if applicable, to the continuation of the meeting on the dates that appear below.

(11)   It is understood that this agreement is limited to the statements made by Client at the meeting and does not apply to any oral, written or recorded statements made by Client at any other time.

(12)   This document embodies the entirety of the agreement between the government and Client to provide information and evidence. No other promises, agreements or understandings exist between Client and the government regarding Client's provision of information or evidence

to the government.

(13) Client and Client's attorney acknowledge that they have read, fully discussed and understand every paragraph and clause in this document and the consequences thereof.

Dated: _August 7, 2018_

At: _Washington, DC_

ROBERT S. MUELLER, III
Special Counsel

By: L. Rush Atkinson
Assistant Special Counsel
The Special Counsel's Office

Michael D. Cohen

Guy Petrillo
Attorney for Client

Dates of Continuation	Initials of counsel, Client and government attorney
9/12/2018	LRA
9/18/2018	LRA
9	

FD-302 (Rev. 5-8-10)

b7E

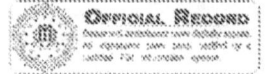

FEDERAL BUREAU OF INVESTIGATION

Date of entry   06/26/2018

Stephen K. Bannon was interviewed at the Special Counsel's Office, located at Patriots Plaza I, 395 E Street SW, Washington, DC. Bannon was accompanied by his attorneys [   ] Present for the interview were Special Agent (SA) [   ] SA [   ] Intelligence Analyst [   ] Senior Counselor to the Special Counsel James L. Quarles, Counselor to the Special Counsel Michael Dreeben, Senior Assistant Special Counselor Andrew Goldstein, Assistant Special Counsel Aaron Zelinsky, and Assistant Special Counsel Elizabeth Prelogar. After being advised of the identity of the interviewing agents and the nature of the interview, Bannon provided the following information:

b6
b7C

b5 per DOJ/OIP

b5 per DOJ/OIP

b5 per DOJ/OIP

b6
b7C

b5 per DOJ/OIP

Investigation on 02/14/2018 at Washington, District Of Columbia, United States (In Person)

File # [   ]   Date drafted 02/26/2018

by [   ]

b6
b7C
b7E

This document contains neither recommendations nor conclusions of the FBI. It is the property of the FBI and is loaned to your agency; it and its contents are not to be distributed outside your agency.

b5 per DOJ/OIP

b5 per DOJ/OIP

b5 per DOJ/OIP

b5 per DOJ/OIP

b5 per DOJ/OIP

b5 per DOJ/OIP

(U) Interview of Stephen K. Bannon (Day
Continuation of FD-302 of 2) _____ , On 02/14/2018 , Page 3 of 37

b5 per DOJ/OIP

b5 per DOJ/OIP

b5 per DOJ/OIP

b5 per DOJ/OIP

b5 per DOJ/OIP

b5 per DOJ/OIP

b5 per DOJ/OIP

b6
b7C

b5 per DOJ/OIP

b6
b7C

b5 per DOJ/OIP

b6
b7C

b5 per DOJ/OIP

b5 per DOJ/OIP

b5 per DOJ/OIP

FD-302a (Rev. 05-08-10)

b7E

(U) Interview of Stephen K. Bannon (Day
2)
Continuation of FD-302 of _____ . On 02/14/2018 , Page 5 of 37

b5 per DOJ/OIP

b5 per DOJ/OIP

After Sessions recused, Trump screamed at McGahn about how weak Sessions
was.   b6
                                                                                             b7C
                       Trump was as mad as Bannon had ever seen him.   b5 per DOJ/OIP

Bannon told Trump Sessions' recusal was not a surprise. He said they had
talked about it back in December.   b5 per DOJ/OIP

b5 per DOJ/OIP

Trump wanted a lawyer like Roy Cohn. He wanted an Attorney General like
Bobby Kennedy.   He thought of them as b5 per DOJ/OIP
people who really protected their President. Trump thought Holder always
stood up for Obama and said Holder even took a contempt charge for Obama
and that Bobby Kennedy always had JFK's back.

b5 per DOJ/OIP

b5 per DOJ/OIP

b5 per DOJ/OIP

b5 per DOJ/OIP

Trump thought he was a winner, he was a fixer, someone who got things done.

b5 per DOJ/OIP

b6
b7C

b5 per DOJ/OIP

b5 per DOJ/OIP

b5 per DOJ/OIP

(U) Interview of Stephen K. Bannon (Day
Continuation of FD-302 of 2) _____ , On 02/14/2018 , Page 7 of 37

b5 per DOJ/OIP

b5 per DOJ/OIP

b5 per DOJ/OIP

b5 per DOJ/OIP

b5 per DOJ/OIP

b5 per DOJ/OIP

b5 per DOJ/OIP

b5 per DOJ/OIP

FD-302a (Rev. 05-08-10)

b5 per DOJ/OIP

b5 per DOJ/OIP

b5 per DOJ/OIP

b5 per DOJ/OIP

b5 per DOJ/OIP

b5 per DOJ/OIP

b5 per DOJ/OIP

b5 per DOJ/OIP

(U) Interview of Stephen K. Bannon (Day 2)

Continuation of FD-302 of _____ , On 02/14/2018 , Page 9 of 37

b5 per DOJ/OIP

b6
b7C

b5 per DOJ/OIP

b5 per DOJ/OIP

b6
b7C

b5 per DOJ/OIP

b5 per DOJ/OIP

b5 per DOJ/OIP

Bannon heard

FD-302a (Rev. 05-08-10)

about conflicts with the Special Counsel from Trump. Trump told him there were issues involving Mueller and Trump's golf course in Northern Virginia, because Mueller had been an equity member at the club but moved and wanted to be cashed out; Mueller was former law partners with [ ] and Mueller was the first person they talked to about serving as the FBI Director. Bannon thought those issues were raised soon after Mueller was named Special Counsel.

b6
b7C

b5 per DOJ/OIP

b5 per DOJ/OIP

b5 per DOJ/OIP

b5 per DOJ/OIP

b5 per DOJ/OIP

b5 per DOJ/OIP

b5 per DOJ/OIP

b5 per DOJ/OIP

b5 per DOJ/OIP

June 2016 Trump Tower Meeting

Bannon had no knowledge of the June 2016 Trump Tower meeting at the time it happened. It was before his time on the campaign. He thought he heard about it from Mark Corallo on a Saturday morning when Trump was en route back to the United States from an overseas trip, or possibly even a day or two before. He heard about it in relation to a media story. Bannon added that before Trump left on the trip, Corallo was in good standing with Trump and Bannon had considered making him Communications Director.

Bannon heard there was an email from Corallo, who mentioned in passing "the lawyers" had an email, or possibly that Marc Kasowitz had gotten an

FD-302a (Rev. 05-08-10)

b7E

(U) Interview of Stephen K. Bannon (Day
Continuation of FD-302 of 2)_____ , On 02/14/2018 , Page 12 of 37

email from a server. Bannon did not go to the G-20 with Trump. He stayed
back to work on the outside law firm. He eventually learned not just their
lawyers had the email but instead "everyone" had it.

b5 per DOJ/OIP

b5 per DOJ/OIP

b5 per DOJ/OIP

b5 per DOJ/OIP

b5 per DOJ/OIP

b5 per DOJ/OIP

b5 per DOJ/OIP

(U) Interview of Stephen K. Bannon (Day

b5 per DOJ/OIP

b5 per DOJ/OIP

b5 per DOJ/OIP

b5 per DOJ/OIP

b5 per DOJ/OIP

FD-302a (Rev. 05-08-10)

b7E

Continuation of FD-302 of
(U) Interview of Stephen K. Bannon (Day
2) _____ , On 02/14/2018 , Page 14 of 37

b5 per DOJ/OIP

Bannon reviewed a document Bates stamped SB_00006329. The Guardian and the Financial Times did articles at the same time linking Felix Sater and Kushner. Bannon knew [Special Counsel prosecutor] Andrew Weissman had put Sater away previously for money laundering.

Bannon knew Kushner was on vacation off the coast of Croatia with a Russian billionaire when Bannon took over the campaign. Kushner was with Wendy Deng, the Russian billionaire, and the Russian's girlfriend. Bannon said his friends in the intelligence community said the girlfriend was "questionable." Bannon called Kushner and told him to come back from vacation. They had 85 days to go, no money and they needed Kushner to come back and fire Paul Manafort.

b5 per DOJ/OIP

b5 per DOJ/OIP

b5 per DOJ/OIP

b5 Per DOJ/OIP

b6
b7C

FD-302a (Rev. 05-08-10)

b7E

(U) Interview of Stephen K. Bannon (Day
Continuation of FD-302 of 2)_____ , On 02/14/2018 , Page 15 of 37

b5 per DOJ/OIP

b5 per DOJ/OIP

b5 per DOJ/OIP

b6
b7C

b5 per DOJ/OIP

b5 per DOJ/OIP

b5 per DOJ/OIP

b5 per DOJ/OIP

b5 per DOJ/OIP

b5 per DOJ/OIP

b5 per DOJ/OIP

b6
b7C

b5 per DOJ/OIP

Bannon first met Trump in August of 2010. Their first meeting was approximately 2 hours long. David Bossie was present and said that Trump was thinking of running for president in 2012. Bannon said "for what country?" It was a 2 hour presentation on a possible presidential run in

2012.   After that, Trump went on Bannon's radio show and did some things
for Breitbart. Bannon had spent approximately 30 minutes combined with
Trump outside of Bannon's radio show approximately 3-4 times.

In 2015 Bannon got to know some of the "outsiders" in the 2016
presidential race, and at that time he got to know [   ] and began   b6
to talk with him quite a bit. Bannon never spoke to [   ] one on one,   b7C
just over the phone. At one point Bannon had spoken to [   ] for
approximately 5 minutes, close to June 2016, on a topic related to
immigration or something similar. Bannon eventually became more in touch
with the presidential campaigns of Ted Cruz, Ben Carson, and Trump. Bannon
did have some conversations over the phone with Corey Lewindowski. Bannon'
s news organization was anti-establishment, so they interacted with that
brand of candidate.

When the presidential primaries ended, Bannon had the same type of
relationship with Trump. Bannon and Trump rarely spoke besides setting up
an interview or Trump coming onto Bannon's show. Bannon was interacting
with populist, anti-establishment camps such as Cruz.

Bannon had read a NYTimes article describing the Trump campaign being in
disarray, so he started to make a few phone calls. At the time, Trump was
12-16 points down, there was talk of the Republican National Committee
(RNC) cutting Trump loose, and the Republicans were talking about
distancing themselves from Trump for fear of losing control of the House
of Representatives. Bannon called [   ] and there was worries   b6
that if Bannon became involved in the Trump campaign, Breitbart could be   b7C
blamed if Trump lost. Bannon had previously talked to [   ]
[   ] back in June 2016 in an effort for them to make peace with Trump.
The [   ] had a Super PAC that was anti-Hillary Clinton and the [   ]
asked how they could help. Bannon wanted to bring KellyAnne Conway and
David Bossie in to help as well. Bannon flew out to Woody Johnson's house
and talked to Trump that night when he arrived. Bannon told Trump he would
take the position as Campaign Chief Executive.

At the time Trump was 16 points down, the campaign had no organization, no
money, 75% of the population thought the country was in decline, they were
working with the "deplorables," and Bannon had a 100% certitude that they
would win. Bannon believed the big task was to give people permission to
vote for Trump as commander in chief.

The next day Bannon met with Manafort, which was the same time that the
news about the "Black Ledger" was breaking. Bannon was at campaign
headquarters when Manafort told Bannon to come up to Trump Tower. When
Bannon arrived, Manafort showed him something about a NY Times story about
the "Black Ledger" and $15 million dollars from the Ukraine. Bannon asked

when this story was coming out. Manafort replied that he had known about
the story coming out for approximately 2 months and had not gotten
involved in it. Bannon subsequently told Trump to keep Manafort, to not
fire him, and to keep him around for a couple of weeks. Bannon called
Kushner, and asked him to get back in order to do something publicity wise
to counteract the negative press surrounding the story. Trump had asked
Bannon at one time about "what was this thing with Manafort out of the
Ukraine," and they talked for approximately 15 minutes on it. Trump was
never linked with other Russian news stories at the time, and he believed
Manafort was a promoter. Trump was more worried about how they story made
them look. Bannon believed that Trump talked with Manafort about the story.

Bannon was involved in all aspects of Trump's debate preparation. Bannon
helped Trump talk and think through various topics related to national
security and foreign policy. The idea of working with Russia to fight ISIS
was "thrown out there". Flynn or Keith Kellogg might have come up with the
idea, with the reasoning that since Russia was dealing with similar
problems in Chechnya, they might be an ally to help. Bannon never
specifically remembered hearing the phrase "knock the hell out of ISIS,"
but that could have become a catch phrase. Overall, Trump had a non-
interventionist stance. During the campaign they were mainly trying to
play defense, it was a very basic strategy, and they were trying to get
Trump to not say something "insane." Flynn might have brought up the idea
of partnering with Russia on fighting ISIS, but not on a geo-strategic
level. Trump's stance was more or less that Russia did not have to be an
enemy.

b5 per DOJ/OIP

b5 per DOJ/OIP

Bannon first met Erik Prince 8 to 9 years ago. Bannon made a film about
Fallujah and he asked Prince to be involved. Bannon wanted to show the
film to Prince for accuracy. The next time Bannon spoke to Prince was when
he came out with a book, "Warrior something." It was approximately 2014-
2015 and Prince had started coming onto Bannon's show.

Bannon and Prince would talk about Islamic radical terrorism. Prince knew
the Middle East, Asia, and sub-Sahara Africa. Prince was a former Navy
SEAL, contractor for the government, and ran his own mercenary company.
Bannon described Prince as a "smart guy." Bannon never really had a
foreign policy talk with Prince for the Trump Campaign, but Prince was not
shy about sharing his ideas.

Bannon was shown Document #1, email dated 9/8/2015 from Prince to Bannon,
subject "Talking Points, second attempt". Bannon stated that he did not
remember passing it along, but it sounded like something he would do.
Bannon was in daily contact with [   ] until he was let go in August.
After that, Bannon would contact Lewandowski nearly every day. Bannon did
not remember discussing the memorandum attached to the email, but said he
would have sent something forward like it.

b6
b7C

Bannon reviewed a document Bates stamped SB-00018818. Bannon stated he did
not remember the email, but it would be something he could have done.
Bannon could not remember if Prince briefed the candidate, but Bannon did
put Prince in contact with Flynn.

Bannon was not in regular contact with Prince. Bannon spoke with Prince a
couple times a month by phone. Prior to Bannon joining the campaign, he
spoke with Prince infrequently. Bannon estimated it to be once a week to
once every couple of weeks. Bannon and Prince would generally talk about
international affairs.

Bannon was shown Document #3, email dated 12/12/2015 from [   ] to
Bannon with [   ] cc'd, subject "Re: Breitbart News." Bannon stated that
[   ] was Breitbart's [   ] Bannon introduced [   ]
to [   ] in order for [   ] to be a source for the article referenced in
the email about data collection.

b6
b7C

Bannon was shown Document #4, email dated 1/14/2016 from Bannon to Prince,
subject [   ] Bannon explained that Prince said he knew people
from his new company. Bannon knew a quality guy from [   ] and he
[   ] Bannon thought that if Bannon
could connect him to some security guys, this guy might be of help. Prince

b6
b7C

FD-302a (Rev. 05-08-10)

b7E

(U) Interview of Stephen K. Bannon (Day
Continuation of FD-302 of 2)_____ . On 02/14/2018 . Page 20 of 37

had connections in the intelligence community that might be looking for
his talents. Bannon did not think that Prince followed up on it.

Bannon was shown Document #5, email dated 3/17/2016 from Prince to Bannon,
subject "Re." From this email, Bannon did not remember if Prince actually
came on his show. Prince was "on the right" and was a highly thought of
guy.

Bannon was shown Document #6, email dated 5/23/2016 from Prince to Bannon,   b6
[   ] cc'd, subject "Fwd: Recommended   b7C
meeting." Bannon did not remember the email exchange. Bannon doesn't
remember meeting with Oleg. Prince viewed Bannon as someone with a good
relationship with Trump.

Bannon was shown Document #7, email dated 10/18/2016 from Prince to
Bannon, subject "Russia/US election." Bannon did not remember this email
or whether he prepared a speech as referenced in the email. Bannon stated
that Prince was not short on ideas. Bannon though the email was more in
reference to Clinton than the Russian influence issue. Bannon thought the
email might be on changing the narrative to Clinton as an alternative to
the stories in the news about Russian election influence. Bannon did not
remember talking to Prince about the email or about talking to Prince
about Russian influence.

Bannon described the 14th floor as "loosy goosy" and Prince might have
come through from August to the Election Day, but he was not certain.
Prince would often have ideas on how he could help them with the debates.
Bannon did not specifically remember how many times he met with Prince at
Trump Tower during the campaign, but estimated it to be a couple of times.
A couple of times Prince would email his ideas to Bannon. Bannon might
have asked for Prince's ideas on a certain issues. Prince knew Conway,
Bossie, [   ] Bannon did not know if Prince provided   b6
advice for any of them. Prince was a known entity in the campaign and   b7C
might have walked around and met people and have come through the 14th
floor. Once someone was on the 14th floor they could walk around freely.
Prince could contact [   ] or someone in security in order to gain access.

Bannon was shown Document #8, email dated 11/16/2016 from Prince to
Bannon, subject "Fwd: Bannon." Bannon didn't remember this email. Bannon
did not know whether Prince was in touch with Mark Corallo. Prince had
just offered his help.

After the election, during the transition timeframe, Bannon continued to
interact with Prince. Prince had come by to speak with Flynn and Bossie
approximately 3 to 4 times. Prince came to New York approximately 5 to 6

FD-302a (Rev. 05-08-10)

Continuation of FD-302 of (U) Interview of Stephen K. Bannon (Day 2) , On 02/14/2018 , Page 21 of 37

times to speak to people other than Bannon such as Flynn, K.T. Mcfarland, Bossie, Kellogg, Conway, [   ] Sebastian Gorka and [   ] Bannon remembered walking by and seeing Prince in the "war room" with [   ] Prince would tell Bannon who he was seeing. Prince would not officially schedule meetings with them. Flynn, Kellogg, Bossie, and Conway had known Prince before then. Prince would come in and sit down and talk about foreign policy. Prince would suggest people they should be getting on board and people to include in the administration. Bannon would bounce ideas off of Prince and talk about such people as Mike Pompeo. The things Prince said were not too crazy and people respected him. Prince had other contacts within the intelligence community. Bannon, Flynn, Bossie and Kellogg had spoken of Prince. Bannon and Flynn had talked with each other about Prince saying he was a good guy.

b6
b7C

Prince came by to see Bannon approximately 3 to 6 times. Prince would come by and talk to one of Bannon's assistants in order to get in. Security at Trump Tower was not overbearing. When they talked, Bannon did talk to Prince about ISIS. Bannon did not particularly remember talking to Prince about Russia in regard to ISIS, but would not be surprised if it came up. Prince did not meet with then candidate Trump, but Bannon thought Prince was close to Eric Trump and Trump Jr. Bannon remembered Prince stopped by during the campaign and asked if Trump Jr was there. Bannon knew Prince would go hunting with Eric Trump and Trump Jr. During the campaign, Prince might have met with Trump Jr, and Bannon remembered that one time Trump Jr might have walked Prince down. Prince met with [   ] [   ] during the campaign as well. Prince always had ideas on what was going on, but Bannon did not remember any of Prince's policy papers making it to Eric Trump or Trump Jr.

b6
b7C

Bannon stated he didn't know Rick Gerson.

b5 per DOJ/OIP

Bannon was involved in the September 2016 meetings with Abdel Fattah El-Sisi and Benjamin Netanyahu. It was Kushner's idea to work toward a summit with Egypt, the UAE, and Saudi Arabia and that Trump would go to this summit in the 1st 6 months of his presidency. MBZ came over as a way to get to know the incoming administration. It was obvious to Bannon that Kushner was told of the meeting prior and had helped set it up. Kushner had talked to MBZ's guys in the U.S. in order to set it up. They met with approximately 25 of the UAE attendees in the lobby, including UAE Ambassador to the U.S. Yousef Al Otaiba, and after approximately 6 to 7 minutes they went up to the penthouse of the Four Seasons. When Bannon walked into the penthouse, he saw another 15 UAE attendees already in the room. Bannon wondered what this meeting could be about. Bannon saw a guy who looked like Sean Connery and realized it was MBZ. MBZ was in jeans and a t-shirt, dressed in casual attire. It was apparent to Bannon that Kushner knew Otaiba and that it wasn't the first time they had met. Bannon believed that the Obama administration had disengaged from the Middle East, which is similar to what El-Sisi and Netanyahu had said. During the meeting with MBZ they discussed the ISIS threat to the area. Bannon did not remember if they discussed Russia, but if they did, it was targeted to the Persian Gulf area. Bannon remembered they talked about Persian expansion, Iran, Baghdad, Beirut, and Hezbollah. The meeting was approximately 2 hours long. Bannon thought that Nader was one of the group of 15 or 25 guys they met as MBZ "held court" for a couple hours. If Nader was there, Bannon believed they just introduced themselves, and shook hands.

b5 per DOJ/OIP

b5 per DOJ/OIP

b6
b7C

FD-302a (Rev. 05-08-10)   b7E

(U) Interview of Stephen K. Bannon (Day
Continuation of FD-302 of 2) _____ . On 02/14/2018 . Page 23 of 37

b5 per DOJ/OIP
Referral/Consult

[   ] had at one time come to Bannon and said he wanted to do something   b6
[   ] Bannon asked [   ] if [   ] was a   b7C
good guy, [   ] Bannon wanted to
know if [   ] Bannon
asked [

[   ] Bannon later found out
that
[   ] Bannon did not recall [   ] talking about [   ] then. Bannon
discussed [   ] was going to go over to
meet with [

Bannon had been working on a proposal to move the Israeli capital to
Jerusalem, the Christian right movement, putting money into a 501(c)(4)
using UAE money or "those guys" which didn't end up happening, and putting
together a security conference over in the Middle East in the Spring
/Summer of 2017. Bannon last saw Nader 2 to 3 months ago. Bannon had too
much going on with the C4 and life in general. Bannon had seen that the
Special Counsel's Office had called Nader to the Grand Jury, but Nader had
not reached out to Bannon.

b5 per DOJ/OIP

Referral/Consult

When shown a photo of Rick Gerson, Bannon stated that this was the college roommate of Kushner, and that he was pretty sure he was the hedge fund guy he referenced earlier. Gerson had a hedge fund on Madison Ave in New York City at Barneys Tower. His office was 2 blocks from Trump Tower on 60th and Madison Ave. Gerson knew a lot about the Middle East and said many intelligent things about it.

b5 per DOJ/OIP

b6
b7C
b5 per DOJ/OIP

Bannon thought he heard that Nader was being called into the Grand Jury for the Special Counsel's Office in the newspaper, but then said that he could be wrong.

b6
b7C
b5 per DOJ/OIP

b5 per DOJ/OIP

b6
b7C
b5 per DOJ/OIP

b5 per DOJ/OIP

b7A Per DOJ/OIP

Continuation of FD-302 of (U) Interview of Stephen K. Bannon (Day 2) _____, On 02/14/2018 , Page 26 of 37

b7A Per DOJ/OIP

b3
Referral/Consult

b3
Referral/Consult

b5 per DOJ/OIP
Referral/Consult

Michael Cohen was one of the lawyers on Trump's staff. Bannon described Cohen as a fixer and a problem solver. In 2010, Cohen came down to the first meeting Bannon had with Trump and introduced himself as a political advisor. When Bannon was on the Trump Campaign, Bannon did not want Cohen wandering around the Trump Campaign organization. Bannon thought it could get them in a lot of trouble since Cohen goes off "halfcocked" a lot. Cohen kept trying to get involved in the Trump Campaign. Bannon described Cohen as the kind of guy who thought it would be a good idea to send $130,000 to Stormy Daniels.

Bannon reviewed a document Bates stamped SB-00013127. Bannon was told "zero" deals involving Russia and the Trump Organization. Candidate Trump would say he didn't know any Russians and there was no collusion. This came up during the campaign a couple of times. Bannon never asked Trump about any Russian business deals. In regard to the emails reference to Felix Sater, Bannon stated that this went back to the House Intelligence Committee, that they had a signed term sheet in December 2015 on Trump Tower Moscow. This was a big deal to Bannon, and Bannon described it as a "big reveal."

b6
b7C
b5 per DOJ/OIP

b5 per DOJ/OIP

b5 per DOJ/OIP

b6
b7C

Bannon was not aware of any financial agreements to Daniels, other
accusers, or other relationships of Trump. Bannon talked to Breitbart guys
about the $130,000 payment, but not to anyone in the administration.
Bannon was not aware of any other payments made. When asked to speculate
about the $130,000 payment Bannon thought it might be David Pecker, since
he did not think anyone around "Trump.org" would be dumb enough, and they
would have worried about the impact to the election.

b5 per DOJ/OIP

Bannon never heard of Cohen arranging for Trump to give a speech on an
online platform or talk about Cohen's concepts for "Trump.org". Bannon had

read a New York Times article about business dealings with Russia and the candidate/"Trump.org". Bannon was aware of the article before he became involved in the Trump campaign. When Bannon was on the Trump campaign, he never discussed the stories that came out involving then candidate Trump during March/April of 2016. During the later stages of the campaign, when the story broke about Trump's house in Palm Beach, Bannon discussed it with Trump and Trump had a plausible explanation. The story never gained any traction. Bannon never talked with Trump on how he thought all these stories on his business dealings with Russia was absurd. The story about Cohen reaching out to Putin's office in January 2016 in order to ask for help on Trump Tower Moscow was a big deal to Bannon and it countered what Bannon heard about Sater by candidate Trump. Bannon did some inquiries about it with his contacts at the Intercept, Fox, the Guardian and ABC News. There was no further information on this, which did not surprise Bannon.

Bannon was shown an email dated 9/28/2016 from Bannon to Cohen with Conway, Kushner, [   ] Stephen Miller, and [   ] cc'd, subject "Re: request from the ft." Bannon did not remember getting an email from Cohen about Sergei Millian, and doesn't remember any conversations about Millian. Bannon never had any conversations with the campaign on the Millian issue.

b6
b7C

b6
b7C
b5 per DOJ/OIP

b5 per DOJ/OIP

Bannon reviewed a document Bates stamped SB-00018384. Bannon did not think this email referenced Cambridge Analytica. Bannon stated that as a private citizen, and lead of Breitbart, he was interested in finding Clinton's

FD-302a (Rev. 05-08-10)

b7E

(U) Interview of Stephen K. Bannon (Day
Continuation of FD-302 of 2)
_____ , On 02/14/2018 , Page 30 of 37

33,000 missing emails. The Government Accountability Institute (GAI) analysis was that the 33,000 missing emails were tied directly to the influence peddling of the State Department. Barbara Leeden knew someone who could work on finding the 33,000 and they had a half a dozen meetings on how to find them. They ascertained that if they would be able to find the emails, they still would not be able to validate their authenticity. They never obtained any emails or any samples and stopped the search. The 33,000 was related to the Clinton Cash book and the pay for play scheme.

Bannon reviewed a document Bates stamped SB-00018418. The green light referenced in the email was for a data operation for voter targeting. There was a presentation about it given to Lewandowski but the data operation people were not retained. Cambridge Analytica then became involved after Ted Cruz officially withdrew in May 2016. In June 2016, [   ] offered an introduction for Bannon to Jared Kushner and Ivanka Trump. Bannon agreed and that was the first time he met Kushner and Ivanka.

b6
b7C

Bannon was shown Document #14, email dated 6/12/2016 from Bannon to [   ] with [   ] cc'd, subject "Re: Defeat Crooked Hillary | [   ] Bannon did not remember sending the email and he never went to the United Kingdom. Bannon did not remember talking to [   ] about meeting with [   ] in general. Bannon would not characterize his response in the email, "Love it," as an approval to [   ] suggestion to meet with [   ] Bannon did not know if [   ] or anyone from Cambridge Analytica, ever reached out to [   ] Bannon thought they probably dropped the idea. Bannon had no idea where [   ] [   ] of Cambridge Analytica and he was focused on getting their data business growing in the U.S. [   ] had a lot of "James Bond" ideas like this idea on [   ] and characterized it as [ ] saying he "knows a guy, who knows a guy."

b6
b7A
b7B per DOJ/OIP
b7C

George Papadopoulos had emailed Bannon during the campaign in an effort to setup a meeting with Egypt. The campaign had decided to take a couple days off during a visit to the U.N. in order to meet with foreign leaders. Bannon was initially against it. Bannon thought Trump's biggest challenge was selling the public that Trump could be Commander in Chief, so therefore he decided to do it and limit the meetings to a few key leaders such as Egypt, Israel, and maybe a couple of others. Kushner wanted a meeting with Israel, and Bannon and Flynn were pushing for a meeting with Egypt. Bannon never worked with Papadopoulos on setting up the meetings despite Papadopoulos's offers through email. Bannon would generally blow off Papadopoulos and thought to himself "I don't need this guy." Flynn would be on the hook for the meetings Papadopoulos was suggesting, and Bannon did not need Papadopoulos. Papadopoulos never told Bannon about the

Russians having dirt on Clinton, and Bannon never heard Papadopoulos tell
anyone else in the campaign, such as Sam Clovis, that the Russians had
dirt on Clinton. Bannon had all the dirt he needed from Clinton Cash and
Uranium One, he didn't need any more dirt. Bannon didn't need any more
dirt from "clowns" like Papadopoulos and Clovis.

b6
b7A
Bannon first met [   ] by email or by phone in 2013-2014 while he was   b7B per DOJ/OIP
working for Breitbart. [   ]   b7C
[   ]
[   ] At the time,
[   ] was running the campaign, and Bannon described it as a "one man
band." Bannon thought [   ] had done "a damn good job." Bannon thought
[   ]

b6
b7A
Bannon was shown Document #15, email dated 1/7/2016 from [   ] to   b7B per DOJ/OIP
Bannon, [   ] subject "Data Guy in Trump Tower."   b7C
Bannon thought [   ] got the wrong name in the email, [   ] who they
got rid of. Giles Parscale had a little data center on the 15th floor.
Bannon was introduced to a "data guy" there in January 2016, but Bannon
didn't remember the name. Bannon speculated that maybe [   ] had some
ideas about it, but Bannon did not think it was [   ] who was involved.

Bannon was shown Document #16, email dated [   ]
[   ]

b6
b7A
b7B per DOJ/OIP
b7C

Bannon was shown Document #17, email dated [   ]
[   ]

b6
b7A
b7B per DOJ/OIP
b7C

In August 2016, Kushner was in charge of the digital campaign and
fundraising. Bannon was the CFO of the campaign with Jeff Dewit. The
campaign had almost no cash and they were receiving only a small amount
from online contributions. The campaign was losing cash at the time and

they were down by a double digit lead with the 1st debate coming.   They
needed $50 million from Trump, which eventually became $10 million.
Afterwards, they were still down by 3 ½ points.

FD-302a (Rev. 05-08-10)

b7E

Continuation of FD-302 of _____ (U) Interview of Stephen K. Bannon (Day 2) _____ . On 02/14/2018 . Page 32 of 37

Bannon was shown an email dated 4/20/2016 from _____ to Bannon and _____ cc'd, subject "Re: Cambridge Analytica." Bannon did not remember this email.

b6
b7A
b7B per DOJ/OIP
b7C

Bannon was shown an email dated 5/04/2016 from _____ to Bannon, subject "[No Subject]." Bannon though this looked like _____ _____ from the email in Document #17. Cambridge Analytica claimed they could help micro-target voters on Facebook. _____ _____ it might have been for a project for Cambridge Analytica.

Bannon was shown Document #18, email dated _____

b6
b7A
b7B per DOJ/OIP
b7C

Bannon was shown Document #19, email dated _____

b6
b7A
b7B per DOJ/OIP
b7C

Bannon was shown Document #20, email dated 8/26/2016 from Bannon to _____ no subject. Bannon stated that _____ _____ Bannon did not remember what the ideas were that he wanted to talk to _____ about referenced in the email. Bannon described _____

b6
b7A
b7B per DOJ/OIP
b7C

Bannon was shown Document #21, email dated 8/30/2016 from Ted Malloch to Bannon with _____ cc'd, subject "The debate." In reference to the email, Bannon stated he had no contact _____ _____ Malloch was a writer and professor at a faculty in London. Bannon knew him from Breitbart London. Bannon did not meet with _____ personally during the campaign, and Bannon felt if he ever would have needed to sit down with _____

b6
b7A
b7B per DOJ/OIP
b7C

Bannon was shown Document #22, email dated _____

FD-302a (Rev. 05-08-10)

b6
b7A
b7B per DOJ/OIP
b7C

Bannon was shown Document #22 again, the email dated [   ]

b6
b7A
b7B per DOJ/OIP
b7C

Bannon was always interested in the missing 33,000 emails, but was not
interested in the John Podesta information since he believed it was not
going to impact the election. Bannon clarified that he was talking to

b6
b7A
b7B per DOJ/OIP
b7C

Bannon was interested in the verified
missing 33,000 emails and how it related to Uranium One. Bannon might have
talked with [   ] at one time, about the 33,000 emails. Bannon did talk
to Candidate Trump about the 33,000 missing emails. After Bannon came onto
the campaign, it got into Candidate Trump's "head" that the 33,000 emails
might be important. Trump was focused on "crooked Hillary" and the Uranium
One story, and thought the 33,000 missing emails might unlock it. They
never discussed that the Russians might have them. Bannon thought that

FBI(19cv1278)-164

some hackers in Bulgaria might have them. There was not much of a response from Trump and every now and then he would bring up the 33,000 emails. One time when the Podesta emails were released, Trump asked if it was a big deal. Bannon [   ] with Trump. Flynn or Kellogg might have had a disc on finding the 33,000 emails. Bannon thought Fly b6 might have had an idea about using an outside company and finding the b7A 33,000 missing emails. If it was anything cyber related, Bannon would b7B per DOJ/OIP always refer them to Parscale and the Cyber guys. Bannon did not think the b7C WikiLeaks releases were that big of a deal, the important information was the 33,000 missing emails. Kellogg thought the same thing, and he was not a cyber guy. Priebus and Miller had talked about the 33,000 missing emails.

After the Billy Bush story broke, one hour later the Podesta emails were released. [   ]
[   ]
[   ] Bannon never thought the Podesta releases were a big deal and they would not have a big impact on the campaign. [   ] b6
[   ] b7A
[   ] b7B per DOJ/OIP
[   ] b7C

Bannon knew [   ] had sent some emails to Bannon. Bannon b6 described [   ] b7C
Bannon didn't take any action in relation to [   ] emails. Bannon did not remember talking to [   ] while he was on the campaign.

[   ] b6
[   ] b7A
[   ] b7B per DOJ/OIP
[   ] b7C
[   ]
[   ]
[   ]

Bannon was shown Document #23, email dated [   ] b6
[   ] b7A
[   ] b7B per DOJ/OIP
[   ] b7C

Bannon was shown Document #25, email dated [   ]
[   ] b6
[   ] b7A
[   ] b7B per DOJ/OIP
[   ] b7C

b6
b7A
b7B per DOJ/OIP
b7C

Bannon was shown Document #26, email dated

b6
b7A
b7B per DOJ/OIP
b7C

Bannon was shown Document #27, email dated 10/22/2016 from Bannon to
and   no subject. Bannon talked to

b6
b7A
b7B per DOJ/OIP
b7C

Prince was going to have fundraiser for Trump and considered it his commitment to the campaign. Bannon did not remember introducing   to any other donors. Bannon did not remember helping any other find funding besides   Bannon was weary of involving himself with   and was only helping out   because he did not want to be "lit up" by   Bannon did not see it as a potential coordination issue working with

b6
b7A
b7B per DOJ/OIP
b7C

Bannon was shown Document #29, email dated 9/21/2016 from Trump Jr to Bannon, Conway, Kushner, Bossie, and   subject "Wikileaks." Bannon did not remember receiving this message, but it was during the campaign timeframe. Bannon did not remember anyone else in contact with WikiLeaks or trying to get in contact with WikiLeaks. There was discussion during the campaign on how WikiLeaks would impact the race. Bannon did not think anyone had any ideas on where WikiLeaks had got their information. Bannon did not remember anyone reaching out to   WikiLeaks, or any other intermediary to see what information might be coming.

Bannon was shown Document #32, email dated 11/5/2016 from Bannon to
Kushner and Bossie, subject "Re; Securing the Victory." Bannon stated that
Manafort had zero involvement in the campaign after he left. Bannon
thought if they responded to this email from Manafort, Manafort would be
telling that to everyone. Bannon was not aware of any instances of   **b6**
Manafort advising, or being involved in the campaign after his ouster. **b7A**
Hicks said he was not involved, and she would have a sense on who Trum**b7B per DOJ/OIP**
talked to. Candidate Trump never said to Bannon that he was in contact **b7C**
with [   ] or Manafort. Bannon knew they were going to win, and in this
email he wanted to avoid Manafort because Bannon believed that if people
could link them to Manafort, they could then try to link them to Russia.

Bannon had three cell phones. He did not use the campaign issued phone or
the "secure phone." The iPad he was issued in the campaign he did not use
much. Bannon was not aware that his cell phone was set up to not archive
text messages, and someone else had setup his phone for him. It was a
surprise to Bannon that his text messages were not archived. During the
campaign and transition timeframe Bannon did not use secure apps. When
Bannon got close to leaving the administration, he got ProtonMail and
Signal. [   ] helped him set up the ProtonMail which Bannon believed   **b6**
provided increased security. Bannon did not use ProtonMail to send or   **b7C**
receive email from people in the administration. Bannon did not have a
Slack channel and never used Slack. Breitbart used Slack, but they were
trying to shut that down. Bannon setup a Wickr account after he left the
administration after Prince talked to him about it being more secure.
Prince talked with Bannon about using Wickr Pro for Breitbart. Bannon used
Wickr with Prince and Signal with [   ]. Bannon only
started using Wickr and Signal after he left the administration. While

Bannon was in the administration, he never heard of anyone using 3rd party
apps. They received a briefing on how their communications needed to be
kept for federal records. Bannon was not sure if his text messages were
supposed to be kept under the federal records act. Bannon did not remember
using his personal phone for White House business. Bannon did not remember
using texting on his government devices, although he might have. Bannon
did not remember any discussion of how his text messages should be saved,
or his personal device texts should be saved. Bannon primarily used the
white house email while he was in the administration. If Bannon received
an email to his "arc-ent" email while he was in the White House, he would
respond to it from the "arc-ent" account. He gave full access to his "arc-
ent" email account to [   ] in order for her to send them to the
White House account to be archived. [   ] might have helped with that as
well.

Administrative:

b7E

The agent notes and documents shown to Bannon will be maintained in the 1A
section of the case file.

2/14/18   Bannon

Dreeben   Quarles
Prelogar   Goldstein
           Zelinsky

b5 per DOJ/OIP

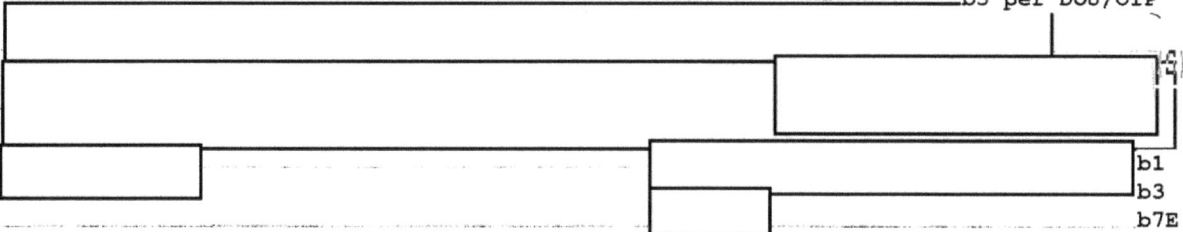

b1
b3
b7E

b5 per DOJ/OIP

b5 per DOJ/OIP

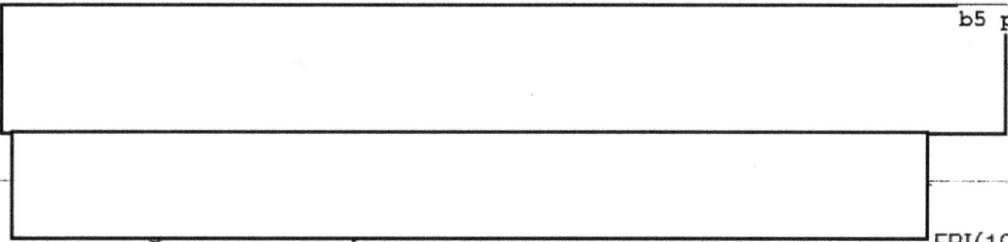

(8)

b5 per DOJ/OIP

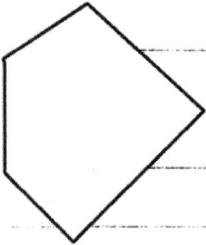

b5 per DOJ/OIP

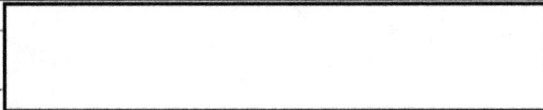

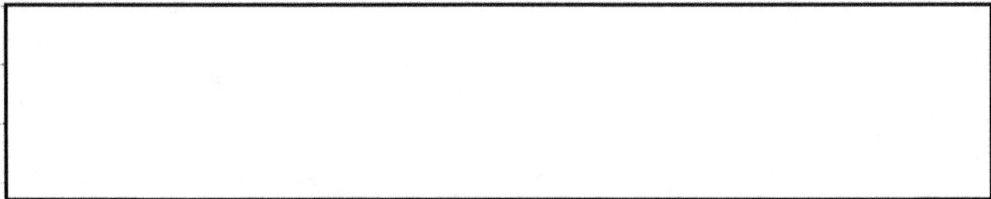

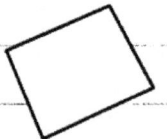

b5 per DOJ/OIP

After recusal, P screaming at McG about
how weak Sessions was.

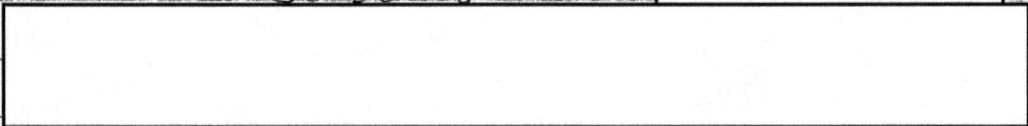

b6
b7C

b5 per DOJ/OIP

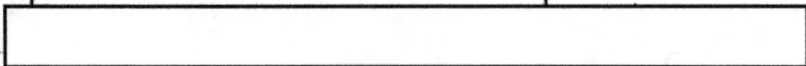 He's as

mad as I've ever seen him.

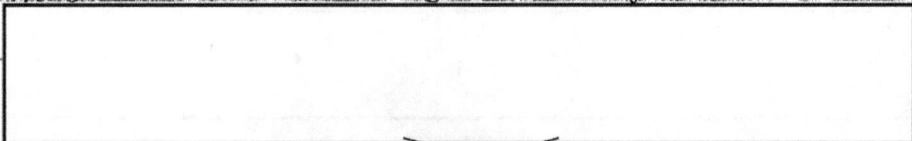

FBI(19cv1278)-176

b5 per DOJ/OIP

SKB: not a surprise. we talked about this, back in December.

b5 per DOJ/OIP

b5 per DOJ/OIP

b5 per DOJ/OIP

b5 per DOJ/OIP

P: wanted in a lawyer — Roy Cohn.
wanted in an AG — Bobby Kennedy.
People that protected
their President. Thought Holder was
always standing up for Obama. Took contempt
charge for ∂.

FBI(19cv1278)-177

(10)

b5 per DOJ/OIP

Bobby K ideal AG. Had JFKs back.

b5 per DOJ/OIP

b5 per DOJ/OIP

b5 per DOJ/OIP

b5 per DOJ/OIP

FBI(19cv1278)-178

b5 per DOJ/OIP

but a fixer, a mnnur, got things done.

b5 per DOJ/OIP

b5 per DOJ/OIP

b5 per DOJ/OIP

b6
b7C

b5 per DOJ/OIP

FBI(19cv1278)-179

⑱

b5 per DOJ/OIP

b5 per DOJ/OIP

conflicts w/ Mueller — heard about it from P.
some situation w/ golf course in NoVa. ① RSM. Equity partner,
moved, wanted cashed out. ② Mueller was former
partner w/ [redacted] ③ first guy talked   b6
to for FBI director.   b7C
I think as soon as named, or shortly thereafter.

b5 per DOJ/OIP

b5 per DOJ/OIP

(2y)

b5 per DOJ/OIP

June 9, 2016 mtg. No knowledge at time.
When did you learn? Think I heard about it from Corallo
on a Sat morning when they were flying backs maybe
a day or two before. Heard about it in relation
to a story.

[Before they left Corallo in good standing w/P.
Thought about making him "Comms director"] b5 per DOJ/OIP

b5 per DOJ/OIP

b5 per DOJ/OIP

recall anything re: email? Heard it from Corallo.
mentioned in passing the lawyers have some email
didn't go to G-20. needed to work on outside ↖
law firm   Kasowitz
                                          pulled something down
                                          from server.

FBI(19cv1278)-189

(22)

Not just our lawyers. Eremones got it.

b5 per DOJ/OIP

b5 per DOJ/OIP

b5 per DOJ/OIP

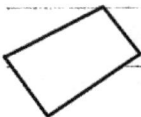

b5 per DOJ/OIP

b5 per DOJ/OIP

b5 per DOJ/OIP

FBI(19cv1278)-190

(26)

b5 per DOJ/OIP

July 24 SB-000006329. Guardian has done an article, FT article same time. Jared, Felix Sater, Andrew W. ___ b6 b7C

JK on vacation off coast of Croatia w/ Russian billionaire when I took over. ___ b5 per DOJ/OIP

I called him and told him to come back.

w/ Wendi Jana, Russian guy and gf ___ Intel say questionable b6 b7C

85 days, no money, got back & fire Manafort

b5 per DOJ/OIP

b5 per DOJ/OIP

FBI(19cv1278)-194

2/14/2018

[ ] Elizabeth   [ ] Aaronz.   Jim Q.   [ ]   b6
                Andrew G.   b7C

met trump Aug. 2010, 2 hours, Dave Bossie said
Trump thinking of running for pres, SB what
country, 2 hr. speculative pres. in 2012
   - Trump on radio show, did some stuff
for Breitbart
   - 30 mins combined,
             outside radio show, 3-4 times
-2015, outsiders con
   - know both Sam Nunbers, → talk more, quote ba
   (had trump on show a bunch of times
   (never one on one, phone
   - never made sure Trump got interviewed,
don't remember one on one conv,
             Sinhs closer to Jure,
             Immigration similar
   - Cruz + Trump, Carsen = became more hostel,
SB news org., anti-establish, on phone with Corey
   - primaries over = same relationship, rarely
spoke Besides setting up an interview w/ his
guys, or coming on his show
             - populist anti-establishment
   camps, Cruz
             ↓   ∨

(1)

FBI(19cv1278)-199

- bolt out of the blue, tie every event to media, media is the real world,
   - NYT, front page article, campaign in dissaray, SB = start making some phone calls, 12-16 points down, RNC cutting him loose, loose House, SB→ call [REDACTED] Breitbart will be blamed. Talked about it, try to have [REDACTED] make peace with Trump back in June, Super PAC, anti-Hillary [REDACTED] how to help, SB, brty Kellyanne, bossie, n.j, flew out to wadj Johnsons house → talked to Trump, Trump→ SB would do it, talked to Trump that night
   - SB - 16 down, no org, no money, 100% certitude you'll win, 75% think country is in decline, deporables, give permission to vote for Trump as commander in chief
   - SB→ met Manafort next dy, news on Black ledger, SB at campaign HQ, Manafort tells SB to come up to T.T, SB shows up, Manafort shows something, NYT story is million from Ukraine, get SB→ when is this coming out? Manafort knows for 2 months, att. said don't get involved, SB→ tell Trump, Manafort not get fired, stay for a couple of week, do what you got to do, Manafort→ think he saw DJT. SB called JK, get back, do something for publicity
   - Trump→ what is this thing, when Manafort fight, is all in, out of ②

b6
b7C

Trump
- never linked with other Russia news
stories. Trump → Manafort is a promoter,
coming into his office.

[redacted]

[redacted]. Trump more worried about the stories
and way it made them look
- SB → involved in all of the debate prep, all
debate prep.
        - National security & foreign policy,
SB helped DJT talk & think through it.
        - working with Russia to fight ISIS,
thrown out there, non-interventionist, Flynn or
Kellogg might have come up, could be an
asset to ally, to help, Chechnya,
        - never remembered using, knock the hell
out of ISIS, could become a catch phrase
        - campaign → playing defense, DJT
not saying something insane, very basic stuff,
Flynn might partner on fighting ISIS, but not
on geo-strategy, Russia doesn't have to be an
enemy

-

[redacted]

③

- 1st met EP 8-9 years ago, SB made a film
about Fallujah, asked EP to be involved, show to
acce,
- next talked, he came out with a book,
warries something, started coming on the show,
14-15

EP + SB
- would talk Islamic radical terrorism,
- EP - he knows the M.E., asia, Sub-Saharan
africa, knows the region, Navy Seal, contractor
mercenary company, smart guy
    - not really had foreign policy talk with
EP for Trump campaign, & EP not shy
about sharing ideas

b5 per DOJ/OIP

Doc 1

[   ]

- don't remember passing along, something he would
do   C.L. [   ] → let go in Aug 1st, SNews) b6 b7C
daily contact, then contacted C.L. every day
don't remember discussing this memorandum,
but said would have sent forward.
                                        something like this

Doc. 2
- don't recall remember, something SB could have
done, don't remember if EP briefed the
candidate, did put him in contact with Flynn

- not regular contact with EP
    - couple times a month by phone
    - prior to joining campaign, infrequently,
once a week → once every couple of weeks
                    - talk about international affairs,
globally,
                ↓

⑤

Dec. 3

- Introduce [REDACTED] b6 b7C
for Breitbart, Info for a source for that
article, [REDACTED] data collection → (same as referenced)

Doc. 4

- EP said he knew people through new company
quality guy from [REDACTED] b6 b7C
[REDACTED] connect to security
guys, could be of help, EP had connections
in free Intel comm, looking for talents don't
think followed

Doc. 5

- don't remember if it took place, EP was on
the right, highly thought of guy

Doc. 6

- not remember this exchange, don't remember
meeting him, EP → viewed SB as someone with
~ good relationship for trump

Doc. 7

- don't remember if he prepared a speech, EP
not short on ideas

b5 per DOJ/OIP

- 14th floor, loosy goosy, EP might have thrown
[REDACTED] election day, not certain
[REDACTED] ideas he could help them with
on debate →

⑥

- SB don't totaly remember, maybe a couple
of times. EP would email a couple of times,
w/ ideas. SB might have asked for new ideas
on certain issues.
- Brought policy ques from ᵘᵖ EP   b6
knew kellyanne,   b7C
EP is a known entity in campaign, might have
walked around, met people, he might have
come through 14th floor, he poked his head in
on Kellyanne, Bossie, don't know if he provide
advice for them, remember him wandering around
talking to bosses, once on 14th floor = could
walk around freely,
- 14th floor, - garners trump security +
14th floor, EP contact [redacted] or secretary
[redacted]

b5 per DOJ/OIP   b6
                                        b7C

Doc.7
- don't remember this email, don't SB think ~~for~~
email is about Hillary Clinton.
- don't think is regarding russian influence
issue, SB about Hillary Clinton, maybe as
an alternative to russian election influence.
- don't remember EP talking about
this, maybe. Don't remember talking to EP about
russian influence
DOC.8 - don't remember

transition

-after election, continue to interact with EP→
come by to talk to Flynn, people to introduce
    - EP= see Flynn, Bossie, 3-4 times
      - coming to New York
       - maybe 5-6, not SB, meet with KT,
[redacted] Kellog, Flynn, SB, Kellyanne,
Dave Bossie, EP would say he would be seeing
them, not officially schedule
        - Flynn, Kellog, Bossie, Kellyanne
knew him before
        - someone is free, EP comes
its it down, talk about foreign policy
people here should be getting on board, ~~Boss~~,
people in the administration
        - SB bounce ideas off of EP
or Pompeo, stuff wasn't too crazy, people
respected him, other contacts in intelligence
        - Flynn + SB, Bossie, Kellog talked
about EP
        - SP/MF about EP, good guy,
EP might have visited with him, guys + ideas
        - Sam with Bossie,   to renovate
KT mcfarland
        - no one else he can think of,
  - EP- 3-6 times coming by
       - came → talk to SB's assistant [redacted] or
[redacted] to get in, security wasn't overbearing

FBI(19cv1278)-206

- did talk with EP & ISIS, Russia in regards to ISIS, not particularly, but wouldn't be surprised if it came up. EP

DOC8

- don't know if EP was in touch with Mark Corallo
[redacted] **b5 per DOJ/OIP**
[redacted] EP just
offered help.

SB thought he was

- EP didn't meet with the candidate, close to Eric & Don Jr. Campaign → EP seeing if Don Jr was there, meet together
    - Kellyanne, Bossie, MF, [redacted] **b6 b7C**
    [redacted] KT mct., Seb Gorkha, Eric, Don Jr. - would likely + see EP, in war room with [redacted]
        - campaign, might have met with [redacted] Don Jr.
Don Jr. might have walked EP down.
        - EP always has ideas on what is going on. Don't remember either way EP → policy papers to the boys

- don't know Rick Grenson
        don't remember

SB involved in Sept
meetings with Sisi + Ben. Net. JK idea to
work through a Summit with Egypt (UAE, saudi)
Trump would go to, in 1st 6 months → related to
this. Walked over. MBZ was coming over as u
get to know us, basic, JK on way or before
Obvious JK told, setup, not # of people.
1 was guys JK talked to MBZ's guys in U.S. to setup.
Some of 25 met in lobby, Yousef, 6-7 meet, took
up to penthouse. walk in and see another 15
guys, SB- what is this, see a guy looks like
Sean Connery → was MBZ, everyone in jeans or
casual attire. JK knew yourself, JK = didn't
feel like first person meet, chief in state officer

FBI(19cv1278)-208

—middle east, Obama admin disengaged, same guys Sisi + Begin met. Kyaid, discussion of ISIS threat to the area. We don't know if discussed Russia, if so tangential, guilt, SB only talk about person expansion, Iran, Baghdad, Beirut Hezbollah, 2 hrs. long.

—think GN met at 25/15 guys key met MBZ "held court" for a couple hours. Just shook hands with SB. Not 100% he was there, just introduced themselves.

①

- GN & mentioned [ ] & came to SB unable to do
something
SB asked [ ] later, was he as good a guy he
came across

b6
b7C

- 4 sensors = mid-December 2016
  - after [ ] called SB everything knew about

b6
b7C

- do not recall [ ] telling about

b6
b7C

[ ] then, [ ] bus. in past, bus. in future.

It

~ Dec mid – Feb meeting²

- don't remember interacting with anyone from the UAE, JK/MP thing, SB3 working on
  ↳ don't remember asking about any Trump officials

~ Petraeus talked about having a better relationship with people in the U.S.
  UAE
    - move capital to Jerusalem, Christian right movement, talked about putting money into CR+C4, UAE money or those guys, didn't end up happening, longer term plan, tie to a security conference over there, banel people between populat!
    - 2-3 months ago - last talked to GN, too much going on with C4, life generally saw SCO called GN to grand jury, he never reached out,

b5 per DOJ/OIP

- discussed ☐ with ☐ on ☐ ›
  going over, meeting with ☐

b6 b7C

b5 per DOJ/OIP

FBI(19cv1278)-211

~approx. 10 minute break

Photo — College roommate of JK, recognized him, pretty sure this photogu

— guy has hedge fund, madison ave, lanes tower, JK came by early, Tony Blair, MF, photo, Nov/December 16, didn't know it was his office, 2 blocks from TT, 60th + Madison Ave.

– GN → GO, thoughts he read it in the paper, JB thought he said it in paper, could be wrong

- MC - One of the lawyers on Trumps staff,
    - MC = a fixer, thought he was a problem
solver 2010 1st
    - 2010, came down to 1st meeting, introduced
as a political advisor
    - mc in Campaign, Monday came down to
SB's office, SB = in trump org., can't be unclass.)
around org/camp. SB → said mc could get
you in a lot of trouble, MC goes off half-cocked a
lot, MC trying to get involved in campaign,
the kind of guy thinking it a good idea to
to send $/130,000 to Stormy Daniels

DOC10 ___

- told zero deals around Russia + Trump org,
Cardinale = know no russians, know no collusion,
Came up during campaign a couple times →
SB → never asked about any Russian bus. deals
    - Felix Sater - SB → this goes back to the
house intel, that they had a signed term sheet
in Dec 15 on Trump Tower Moscow, Big deal
to SB,   ↓ in T.T., but reveal to SB   b5 per DOJ/OIP

SB- ~~Not~~ aware of any financial agreements,
to Stormy Daniels, accussers, or relationships
of DJT

    - SB talked to Breitbar guys about 130k
payments, not to administration

    -not aware of any other payments
made

    -130k speculate, SB thought it msn
be David Pecker → anther.... didn't think
anyone around Trump org. would be close enough,
to impact the election.

- never heard of M.C. arranging for DJT to
arrange for a speech on an online platform,
M.C. talk about concepts for Trump Org.
- SB → NYT about bus. dealings w/the Russia
+ Trump Org. / Charlotte

Felix Sater was telephone contact, SB was
aware of before becoming involved

SB didn't discuss when was on campaign

Stories came + went March April 2016,

- later stages of campaign, house in
Palm Beach, didn't get any traction. Never
discussed with Candidate on Palm Beach house,
had a plausible explanation.

b6
b7C

b5 per DOJ/OIP

8.

- SB - never remember getting email, don't remem
any Conv. about S.M., no discussion w/int campaign
on S.M. issue.

b5 per DOJ/OIP

b6
b7C

b5 per DOJ/OIP

b6
b7C

→ reaching to Putin's office in Jan. 16, help,
reveal

- me was a big deal to SB, countered what
heard about F.S. by the candidate

– SB did some inquiries, the intercept,
fox, the guardian, abc news, & they trying to
track down

– know FS to, so not surprised again.

– break, approx 15 mins

– CA, May 2015
  – vice Chairman + owned 2 1/2 %, up to 5 option
  – didn't speak to [ ] or infreq., in that time
period.

Dec 12
  – think this is not CA, Barbara LaBeen
    – Clinton Cash may 15, FOIA request comes
through 33,000 missing, GAE analysis,
33,000 → tie Directly to influence peddling at
State department, SB open to meeting as
private citizen + head of Breitbart, Barbara → knows
a guy, 1/2 dozen meetings to how get 33,000 emails,
ascertain can get, not validate. didn't get any or samples
stopped search
                      related to
33,000 → Clinton Cash, Pay for play
                      book

Dec 13
  – green light = data operation for voter targeting,
Corey presentation, was not retained, people
To Corey

—CA involved, after Cruz officially withdraws→
      —around June, offers into [REDACTED b6 b7C] do

Paul & Ivanka, 1st time SB met Paul &
   Ivanka, said fine, present pro
    —no

Doc. 14

   — doing remember sending it, never went to cts,
  or whatever don't remember talking to [REDACTED b6 b7A b7B per DOJ/OIP b7C] about it,
    — wouldn't characterize as an approval, don't know, if
[REDACTED] reached out
        —June = not familiar with CA trying to
   get in touch with [REDACTED]
          —probably dropped
       —No idea where [REDACTED]
   — [REDACTED] CA, focus on getting about bus, in
U.S, all a little bit fantasist, ba like James bond,→
ideas like this on [REDACTED] knows a guy who knows a
guy

  — GP — during transition, not remember talks about
    Egypt, campaign → GP emails trying to get involved
  in setting up the meetings
      — campaign, made a decision, to
take a couple days off during U.N. visit & meet
foreign leaders, SB was against, in C.I.C, self,
H.C. committed to it, limit it to Egypt, Israel,
maybe a couple others. JK→Israel, SB/MF, ⑤
             Egypt

- Not ur truth GP on twns
- Committee in March [blank], called [blank], why put
13th out, nobody knows GP → point it out,
           sessions, schang   model U.N.
blamed S.C.
           - GP email chain, thought GP was
George Gigrest, SB → gently blowing GP off,
SB → I don't need this guy, MR will be on the
hook for it, don't need GP

- GP - never told SB about Russians having
    dirt on Clinton or anyone else in campaign,
    or show clout.
           - SB - had all the dirt of Clinton cash,
    wanted one, we didn't need any more
    clowns like GP & SC, that's real dirt
           GP
           - didn't hear anyone talk about

b6
b7A
b7B per DOJ/OIP
b7C

- 1st met [blank]
           - by email or phone, 13, 14, on breitbars,

—Silverberg = ranke thing, one camp,
man bowl, did a damn good job,

Docs

— think he has the wrong name there, [ ] who
they got rid of, Parscale, → little data center
on 15th floor,

— introduce to data guy, don't
remember, Jan 16, maybe [ ] had
some ideas about it

— [A] not think its [ ]

(27)

— aug 2016

— money situation = JK was in charge of digital
and fundraising, SB→ CFO of campaign. Sunday
Jeff Dewitt

night meetings, had almost no cash, only small
from online, loosing cash, close by double digit,
1st debate coming, need $50 million from Trump
becomes $10 million from Trump. was still down, 3½
down.

email into

— don't remember this

email text received from

— looks like   CA. can help micro target
on Facebook   might be a
project for CA.
project

(28)

Doc 20

Don't remember when S

wanted to talk w/him.

— Mifflloch — suggests he's a writer, breitbart/ubla,
professor on faculty in London, later

Doc 21

— No Contact w/S

— didn't meet personally w/him [ ] during campaign
eya — need to sit down

(29)

[redacted]

b6
b7A
b7B per DOJ/OIP
b7C

[redacted]

- break 10-15 minutes

email - 1st in time

[redacted]

b6
b7A
b7B per DOJ/OIP
b7C

[redacted]

b6
b7A
b7B per DOJ/OIP
b7C

[redacted]

170

b6
b7A
b7B per DOJ/OIP
b7C

b6
b7A
b7B per DOJ/OIP
b7C

SB→ alums)

Interested about 37,000, not interested in protests
not going to impact

~ gross tweets
~

b6
b7A
b7B per DOJ/OIP
b7C

~ pers belief

(31)

may have told SB→ Aug fundrs campaign
not at presbrtrl

[redacted]

b6
b7A
b7B per DOJ/OIP
b7C

- SB→ interest in verified 33,000
emails related to uranium one
- 33,000, talked to ~~candidates~~
candidates,

manafort story before went right to Clinton
cash + uranium one. SB→ said it was
way too late
- after came on campaign, got into
WJB head 33,000 emails important + Steven
Miller, DJT was focused on crooked Hillary
and uranium one, 33,000 unsure might unlock
it. Didn't think yet in that timeframe,
never discussed that Russians could have
had it, SB→ spent some time, hackers in
hackers might have it   Bulgaria
                              might have it

DJT→ not much of a response, every now
+ then he would bring up 33,000. One time
Podesta emails released - is this a big deal

b6
b7A
b7B per DOJ/OIP
b7C

[redacted]

- No attempts to get 33,000 during campaign (32)
unverifiable

FBI(19cv1278)-232

- might have had RNC on finding 33,000
emails, MF, Kellog
   ↳ don't remember, might have
      - SB- releases, not that big of a
deal, important 33,000 emails
         - Kellog = same shtt, not a cyber guy
      Renee
              ⟶ talked about

      - email - much ado about nothing
Campaign think MF might have an idea/company, not
after labor sure emails, something about cyber, SB⟶
day, ~~still~~ talk to Parscale/cyberguys
      still

   - digital guys, talk to them,
         brought Anasco, by on 13th,
   meeting with MF maybe someone else, Parscale,
   small parscale digital offices, don't know if
   anything came out of it,

- Billy Bush, 1 hour later Podesta emails came out,
   tape   SB⟶ thought built up to Podesta

         ↓

- 55 mins, 3 - call, 4 - came out Billy Bush
type, called wash post, SB give us audio,
we can verify on Monday,
     - got transcript the oah a called
general counsel, was quick

- knows

July 25th
2016

     - sends email to SB

- didn't take any action related to this
- don't remember talking to [ ] on campaign

(34)

DOT
- I don't talk w/ DOT Russia, I have 33,000 enruts release candidate -
   - If they care at would have an interest

DOC27

SB→ asked

— ER was going to have a
fund raiser for Trump→ W3 Commianamoo

don't know a

— don't remember introducing ____ to any other donors
maybe
— don't think ____ ever met with her
— don't remember helping others with funds, besides
____, didn't want to be led up, remote chances,
SB→

(37)

FBI(19cv1278)-237

- SB - didn't see it as a potential coordination
issue with [redacted]

    - try to show enough respect

[redacted boxes]

Doc 29

- don't remember receiving this message, campaign,
don't know if anyone else in contact
with wikileaks or btry trying to get in contact
    or trying
      - discussion on wikileaks = how this   yes
    will impact or whatever, in campaign
      - don't think anyone had any idea on
where they came from, how they got
SB or [redacted]   - don't remember reaching out to [box] or
WMc, or interacting to see what information
might be coming.

Doc 33

- Manafort had zero involvement in campaign
    - if response to this than PM will be
telling everyone
    - not aware PM was advising involved in
campaign after his ouster
    - HH said weren't, sense on who he
talked to, candidate - nothing said about [box] or PM

(38)

3ᴵ

- SB knew they were going to him,
    – wasn't mainly a direct connection
  maybe, link to manafort, could be linked
  to Russia worked to

- 3 phones
    - just those 3   didn't use
        - campaign phone, secure phone
        - the ipad = doln't use much, drudge
    - phone not aware phone setup to not archive
  text x text messages, not aware, guy who
  setup, was a surprise
    - Campaign
        - no secure apps >,
    - transition
        - NO) slack, whats app, wicker
    - got close to leaving administration
        - Setup proton mail, signal
            ∨> ███████████████████   b6
                                                        b7C
        - proton mail, increased security,
  not from people in admin, didn't use or
  receive,

- not a lot of people / only former

- not used at receive [with similar after] / no admin current / not used in admin / couple weeks

        - slack, did not have a ~~the~~ slack channel
  never used slack, Breitbart used = trying to shut down
        - wicker – EP talking about secure,
  Setup after left admin,
        - Signal   Signal   based on security
    └ ∓ EP → wicker, ███████████████   b6
                                                        b7C

(39)

FBI(19cv1278)-239

- in admin - not know of anyone using 3rd party
  - briefing, federal records, keep these,
  - text messages = don't remember should
keep and Federal records → ~~another~~ act
    - personal + white house email's
    - don't remember using personal phone
text for W.H. business →
    - don't remem. textrun on gov't devices, text
on personal devices, might have, don't remember,
never heard text messages should be saved,
    discussion,
    - or personal device texts should be
saved
8/20/2017
    - ED → wickr pro for Breitbart

- primarily used the white house email in administration
    - sent, new people on white house,
    - arc-ont if got there, to respond on account
gave to ~~official~~ official to assistant to send to
    [redacted]   b6
                                                                    b7C
  white house account for archived
- didn't think about text messages, ~~personal~~ → to be archived,
  didn't think about, don't remember, if text message
qualified under federal records act

(40)

FBI(19cv1278)-240

– think remember [ ] or [ ] to look at the
SB's emails to archive,

– [ ] had access to ancient emails,
SB gave her full access

From: [   ] Breitbart   b6
Sent: Mon 7/24/2017 5:05 PM (GMT-04:00)   b7C
To: Steve Bannon
Cc:
Bcc:
Subject: Re: Jared Kushner sealed real estate deal with oligarch's firm cited in money-laundering case |
        US news | The Guardian

How do we prove that

That's game set match

Sent from my iPhone

On Jul 24, 2017, at 5:01 PM, Steve Bannon [   ] wrote: b6
                                                       b7C

 Dude !!!

  On Jul 24, 2017, at 4:30 PM, [   ] Breitbart [   ] wrote:

  Wtf!!!!

  Sent from my iPhone

  On Jul 24, 2017, at 4:26 PM, Steve Bannon [   ] wrote:

  He was on 'vacation' off the coast of Croatia with a Russian billionaire when I took over
  campaign

    On Jul 24, 2017, at 4:23 PM, [   ] Breitbart [   ] wrote: b6
                                                           b7C

    A progressive activist w ties to pelosi told me that

    Don't know if true

    Sent from my iPhone

    On Jul 24, 2017, at 4:21 PM, Steve Bannon [   ] wrote:

    WTF

    On Jul 24, 2017, at 3:04 PM, [   ] Breitbart [   ] wrote:

    I heard he had a meeting w WIKILEAKS in Europe last year. Nothing to verify yet but I
    heard it happened from a fairly reliable source. Just FYI.

    Sent from my iPhone

On Jul 24, 2017, at 3:01 PM, Steve Bannon ⟨   ⟩ wrote:

All and everything

On Jul 24, 2017, at 2:59 PM,   wrote:

k this is big though isn't it? It's the ball game...

Thanks
[   ] Breitbart News

-----Original Message-----
From: "Steve Bannon" [   ]
Sent: Monday, July 24, 2017 2:49pm
To:[   ]
Subject: Jared Kushner sealed real estate deal with oligarch's firm cited in
money-laundering case | US news | The Guardian

https://www.google.com/amp/s/amp.theguardian.com/us-news/2017/jul/24/jared-
kushner-new-york-russia-money-laundering

Don't touch yet

From: Erik Prince ▮▮▮▮▮▮▮▮▮▮▮▮▮▮
To: Steve Bannon ▮▮▮▮▮▮▮▮▮▮
Cc:
Bcc: ▮▮▮▮▮▮▮▮▮▮▮▮▮▮▮▮

Subject: Talking Points, second attempt
Date: Tue Sep 08 2015 00:59:37 EDT
Attachments: Talking Points.pdf
Untitled attachment 37411.txt

b6
b7C

MEMORANDUM

FROM ERIK PRINCE
TO: TRUMP CAMPAIGN
VIA: STEVE BANNON
SUBJECT: Defense and Foreign policy talking points

IRAN

It is important to note that the "Arab Spring" actually started in Persia in June of 2009, long before protests in elsewhere . Throughout Iran there were at least 2 million people in the streets protesting the Regime and demanding political economic and social freedoms. All the people on the streets needed was a little verbal encouragement from the West but none was forthcoming. Total Silence from Washington. The Iranian regime was so in peril that they didn't even trust their own Iranian forces to come in and crack down on the protests but instead imported Lebanese Hezbollah surrogates to come in and break up the protests, murdering, arresting and hanging their way to success.

The Middle East is now experiencing a full on Sunni vs. Shia war. KSA (Saudis) are threatened as the "capital" of Sunni Islam and defender of the Holy Places of Mecca and Medina. The Iranian/ Persian military dictatorship is fully engaged to dominate and enjoy hegemony over the entire region in a way not experienced since the Persian empires of the 7th and 8 Centuries. Persia was originally "islamized" by the Arabs and the Sunni vs Shia contest has simmered or boiled since then. We are now in an intense period of boiling, only to be exacerbated by the horrible Nuclear Deal negotiated or actually capitulated by the Obama Administration. The goal of Iran from the beginning is to drive the US from the Middle East and dominate the vacuum remaining. With nuclear weapons and the considerable bonus of the released Sanction funds the Iranian Regime will be well primed to continue their strategy. They are a very deliberate people. This is a society that places up to a thousand stitches in a square inch of a Persian rug. **They have been focused on a path to regional dominance and they are winning.**

Since the 1979 Iranian Revolution the Iranians have been building and exercising their unconventional warfare capabilities. **Qassem Sulimani** runs the Quds force which is the Special Forces Unit of the **Iranian Revolutionary Guards Force.** The IRGC is really the military dictatorship of Iran. They dominate the entire Iranian society and Armed Forces just like the SS dominated the entire society and Wehrmacht (German Army) of Hitler's Third Reich. Qasem Soleimani is the Heinrich Himmler of the Iranian State. He is the muscle that keeps the Supreme Leader Ayatollah Khameni of Iran in power. The 12 man Guardian Council is their inner circle and effectively chooses any candidates for power. Rouhani may be the President of Iran but the real power is the Supreme leader and the Guardian Council. Soleimani is their muscle.

The Quds Force is the worldwide special operations arm that's very effective at its asymmetric and surrogate warfare mission. It is how the Iranians dominate Lebanon (and threaten the north of Israel) through their Shia proxy Hezbollah(Hizb Allah- Party of God, leader **Hassan Nasrallah**). Hamas (Leader: **Khaled Meshaal)** in the Gaza Strip is their Palestinian Proxy and who fires all the rockets and sends suicide bombers to Israeli civilian targets. (Hamas is Sunni but still their hate tool against Israel). It is also how the Iranians dictate/support Iraq though Shia Militias, and the Houthis (also a Shia minority group in Yemen).

The Quds Force has been killing Americans from the very beginning. Their sponsored major terror acts include blowing up the U.S. Embassy in Lebanon, the Marine Barracks bombing in 1983 (241 USMC killed in action), kidnaping torture and murder of CIA Station chief Buckley (they even sent the torture tape to Langley), numerous other kidnappings and bombings against American and Israeli targets. Of late it is the Quds Force that supplied Iraqi Shia extremists with a extremely dangerous Improvised Explosive Device IED (road side bomb) called an EFP- Explosive Formed Penetrator which slices through almost all US armor and causes hideous injuries and death to the vehicle occupants. The Iranians have killed and maimed thousands of Americans in Iraq and Afghanistan. That Soleimani and his ilk are not already DEAD is a national disgrace for America.

SYRIA

It is via a combination of Lebanese Hezbollah and IRGC troops that Iran supports Bashar Assad directly in Syria. Iran supports Assad in Syria because Syria was the logistics bridge by which Iran has flowed all the weaponry into Lebanon over the last 35 years. It is also a matter of Shia Solidarity. The Hafez Assad Bath Party Regime took power in 1970 by force. It is an aberration in Syrian history since The Assad family is Alawite, a Sect of Shia Islam. Alawites represent only 12% of the population and were long persecuted by the majority urban Sunnis. It would be like a Dalit/Untouchable becoming President of India. The Sunnis in turn for the last 45 years were persecuted and kept in check by force. When Hafez Assad died, his son Bashar was not in the family dictatorship business at all. He was a dentist living in London and leading a normal life with an attractive, western dressing wife. He quite reluctantly returned to run the country and actually made a number of entreaties to the U.S. wanting to improve relations. As the Arab Spring chaos spread to Syria the Sunnis leapt at the chance to resist. The Alawite dominated army backed by Soviet/Russian weapons tried to crush all resistance with conventional power of armor/artillery and carpet bombing causing massive carnage and starting the largest refugee crisis in Europe since WWII. There have been massive casualties suffered on both sides. It is estimated that 1 of every 3 Alawite males of military age have already been killed in the fighting. It is a blood and religious feud without any chance of peaceful resolution while ISIS or other radical Sunni forces exist. Assad cannot capitulate because if he leaves or loses it is a war of Tribal Extinction. The coastal living Alawites of Syria would be en masse slaughtered. The solution for Syria is inextricably linked to Iraq.

IRAQ

Iraq was dominated for decades by another Bath Party member, in this case a Sunni named Saddam Hussein. His removal caused great hope for the Shia majority in the south, the persecuted Kurds in the north and wariness among the Sunnis in the middle and west of the country. Democratic elections in the country were ill advised as they were bought and paid for by Quds Force money and intimidation throughout the Shia south especially. The Mahdi Army and Badr Corps became the lead surrogates among the many Shia militias in Iraq. They quickly became more organized and formidable than the Viet Cong ever were in Vietnam. They were the tool used to infiltrate and dominate the levers of power in Iraq. They effectively purged Sunnis from Baghdad and from the spectrum of security organizations. The premature pullout of US forces unleashed Shia extremism and caused the beleaguered Sunnis of Iraq to make the Faustian bargain to cooperate with ISIS who promised to protect them from Shia aggression. When ISIS rolled into northern Iraq they captured 5 heavy divisions of Iraqi army equipment and

3 major logistics bases stocked with US made ordnance, supplied and funded by the U.S. Taxpayers.

ISIS is a very adaptive and clever foe. The recent U.S. Drone strike is the first of its kind against a computer hacker. That the USG needs to marshal its forces to kill their hacker is indicative of their growing and not receding capabilities.

They flow very smoothly from small 2-4 man terror cell teams up to 1,000 man or more conventional fast moving light cavalry operations. Although they have no airpower they still have precision strike capabilities. They utilize an armored vehicle loaded with explosives and a suicide driver to deliver ordnance on call for their commanders, keeping a number of prepped vehicles on call for immediate response to the tempo of combat.

They see exactly how the U.S. playbook reads and they have adapted to it and are largely unfazed by it. They have an unprecedented incoming supply of recruits because for Islamic Extremists, Syria is the Super Bowl of Jihad. Young jihadis showed up to fight in Afghanistan against the USSR then the USA, they came to Iraq for Jihad but Syria is their main event for all eternity. For every loser seeking meaning in their life that's dabbled in Koranic studies, they find all the prophesy they need to support an Isis Caliphate. Isis provides them with training, equipment, income and a steady supply of the spoils of war to fulfill their sickest fantasies. **Abu Bakr al-Baghdadi,** is a serious player and has taken an Al Qaeda business model to the next generation. He's an Islamic scholar thats quite adept at building an organization that governs, recruits and advances its goals. While AQ was a dispersed terror organ, ISIS is a terror state with increasingly global reach that also holds a large amount of terrain, equipment and ongoing revenue streams ranging from crude oil, kidnapping and extortion. They derive legitimacy by surviving in the face of the feckless efforts to defeat them. Their lean and dispersed command structure allows for rapid decision making and limits damage caused by the occasional successful USG drone strike. They have a world class communications and social media outreach that serves to promote their brand and aid in recruiting. Their monthly online newsletter Dabiq is widely enough consumed across the worlds 1.5 billion Muslim population to cause a worrying stream of incoming recruits.

The newsletter is named for a city north east of Allepo in Syria. The are numerous Koranic end time prophesies about the last great battle that will occur in Dabiq where the armies of Jihad defeat the army of the north (Christendom). A bold move by the Next President would be to give them the fight they so desperately seek. Moving a couple thousand US marines nearby Dabiq, in a position to threaten the city would be a bait that ISIS couldn't resist, like flies to a lantern. The U.S. is frankly lousy at counterinsurgency but does industrial level war very well. Let the small American force hold out defensively for a few months while ISIS moves more into the area and then unload on them with everything non nuclear we have. (24/7 B-52's, Fuel Air Explosives, artillery, rockets, cluster bombs, etcetera). Kill everything in every grid square surrounding those Marines, while also flattening Dresden style their Caliphate capital of Raqqa Syria. Nothing will be as demotivating for their recruiting efforts is well publicized video of total destruction of their forces. As gruesome as that may sound, they think with medieval perspective and you must give them a pounding they will understand.

The long term solution is to adjust the map of the Levant. When the U.S. pulled out of Iraq the country was still intact. The absence of US presence unleashed the Shia extremism instigated by Quds forces. The Iraqi PM Malaki fired countless competent Sunnis from the Intel Service,

Army and Interior Ministry. This truly disenfranchised the Sunnis who found themselves without jobs, income, electricity or protection. When Isis was active across the border, the Sunni tribes made the Faustian bargain to cooperate with Isis since the Shia were treating them horribly already. The Sunni mistake is obvious and they will never ever reconcile with Shia run Baghdad. Neither will the Kurds who are consistently deprived of weapons and oil funds they are due, ever want to stay part of Iran/Shia dominated Iraq.

Assad in Syria has already indicated he's willing to have a power sharing agreement. It is time to undo the WWI era Sykes-Picot agreement drafted by the French and British. That map was drawn for their colonial interest and not based on any tribal or cultural logic. The USA should provide real leadership and support the redrawing of the levant borders once and for all. Accept that Syria and Iraq are done even though it's theoretically possible to rebuild a shattered glass vase, the expense in blood and treasure has already been far too high.

A free and independent Kurdistan is the first place to start. The Kurds could unify the northern part of existing Syria all the way to the Mediterranean sea. Kurds are already halfway there by already taking Khobani Syria. Nineveh province would become a long needed Christian homeland adjacent to Kurdistan. A unified Sunni nation consisting of western Iraq and eastern Syria. Arming the Kurds and the Sunni tribes in their own homelands would eliminate the sanctuaries where Isis can exist and thrive. Isis can be destroyed with conventional combat power either fielded by the U.S. and Arab allies or it can all be rented from private contracted forces to fight alongside Arab neighbors and the indigenous civilized populations. Once the large scale conventional Isis capabilities are annihilated, the isolation and elimination will be simpler among unfriendly populations defending their lands.

Finally, Lebanon has been a battered state since WWI, enduring a famine induced by the Turks that killed over 200,000 and wars, assassinations and non stop strife. Lebanon is effectively a rump state where the Iranian sponsored and heavily armed Hezbollah militia hold complete sway over the impotent government. (Hezbollah are the guys that fought the Israeli Defense Force to a standstill in 2006). Let the Shia parts of Lebanon go with Assad and the Alawites along the coast.

Sadly it's necessary to reorganize the troubled neighborhood that is the Middle East. Absent some clear actions, the world will be dealing with second and third order metastasis from a Caliphate growing stronger every month

As one considers how the country defends itself going forward, some perspective how we got here as a nation is needed. The tools of warfare have advanced rapidly and some mistake that changes in Tech mean the old facts of war: deceit, fear, casualties and annihilation are past. They aren't. Some brief history:

Generations of War
First Gen: Moves at the speed of foot/horse, no electronic communications. Linear war. American Rev and Napoleonic Wars

Second Gen: Trench warfare, Little maneuver. Industrial slaughter. Begin automatic weapons (American Civil war and WW1)

Third Gen Warfare: Blitzkrieg, maneuver on sea air and land. (carrier battle groups, strategic nuclear triad and Combined Air land battle doctrine) What the USG trained and equipped for the entire Cold War and what the entire military industrial complex still wants to fight. Very high cost and exhausting, cannot be sustained for long periods. (Gulf War 1, 2003 Iraq invasion)

Fourth Gen Warfare: Non state actors organize the proliferation of commercial Technology that just 20 years ago was highly classified. (Using Google earth to plan base mortar and rocket attacks, more computing power in an iPhone than aboard Apollo 11) The 9/11attacks utilized the most cost effective weapon system in history, box cutter knives and suicide fanatics. A $500k attack has cost the U.S. taxpayer trillions and surrendered liberty. The USG is still fighting its current challenges of surrogate warfare with all its 3rd gen warfare gear, tactics and mindset.

The USG has mastered the most expensive ways to wage war. The defense and intel budgets consume more funds than the next seventeen countries combined. **We effectively try to mow the lawn with a brand new Rolls Royce.**

Examples: the Lockheed Martin F-35 is the most expensive weapon system in the history ($1.4 Trillion for program duration) of the world. Read the article it will explain how badly politicized the acquisitions process has become. The F-35 is built in 45 of 50 states but despite its bright claims its way behind where it should be. There was a recent dogfight fly off between a 30 year old F-16 carrying two large drop fuel tanks vs. a clean configured new F-35. Result: old F-16 spanked the shiny new F-35. All these shiny expensive tools have no role fighting a 4th Gen foe.

http://www.vanityfair.com/news/2013/09/joint-strike-fighter-lockheed-martin

I can bore you with examples if you want to read further...

What this means is that trying to fight a 4th Gen war with our 3rd Gen Military is exhaustingly expensive and ineffective since it prevents the adaptation needed to out innovate the 4th Gen foe. We have bureaucratized warfare to an unparalleled level and the cost exhaustion and failures in Iraq and Afghanistan bear witness. We still have more Admirals than Navy ships. We have allowed lawyers to second guess every decision made by field commander. If troops need Close Air Support while fighting in Afghanistan, they shouldn't need to ask permission from a U.S. lawyer sitting in Qatar.

There are a host of ways to fight 4th Gen wars better and ways to cut massive amounts of fat out of the defense budget but we can wait till after the election for that. More defense spending isn't needed, better leaders and smarter spending is. When you have a failing investment, any smart investor doesn't throw more money at the problem. Instead you change leadership and the business plan. All of Washington will tell you to spend spend more, we all know how consistently wrong their paradigm is...

Why does Russia care about Syria and Iran?
Syria and Iran have remained the most consistent client states of Russia since Assad took over in 1970 and the Iranian Revolution in 1979. They are significant weapons customers and the Syrian Port of Tartuz provides Russia their Mediterranean Navy Port.

A little known fact is that the Iranian Supreme Leader Ayatollah Khameni attended the Patrice Lumumba Univ. In 1983 in Moscow which was the primary recruiting ground of the KGB. He's had a closeness to the Russian Security service ever since. The recent deployment of Russian troops were primarily Forces from Eastern Ukraine that sided with Russia when Putin started his surrogate war. Now that the abuse of all Ukraine has continued those troops loyalty to Russia is suspect so he solved two problems sending them to Syria.

Afghanistan: The country is consistently failing further and further. The U.S. and allies have created a completely welfare nation. The Afghans have no ability to generate sufficient revenues to provide any level of government service, let alone their expensive military built in the image of the U.S. Army. The list of failures and errors are too long to catalogue here. It is salvageable but with a low cost approach more in keeping with the British East India Company and not how the U.S. Military has blown through a Trillion dollars over 14 years with little to show. The private model to Afghan security may be too much for people to handle but at least budgetary discipline must be imbued to the field decision makers just like authority and responsibility must be pushed down to the lowest possible level.

China

As a country the PRC has a real problem with Islamic terrorism. It is an area we can be working closely with them as they have problems that leak into China from Afghanistan. In the northwest province if Xinjiang which borders Afghanistan lives a non ethnic Chinese minority's called the Uighurs (pronounced: We -Wers). They consistently have committed some large acts of terrorism from truck bombs, driving fast through a market with a truck, a multi attacker knife fight in a train station that killed 29 people etc. the government responds with a very heavy hand. Also there's been controversy about the PRC claiming entire regions of the South China Sea as territorial waters including waters belonging to their neighbors. They stake their claim by building dredged islands with ports and airfields on the newly created land. Much of this provocation causes internal strife between the party and the PLA. These unnecessary moves are easily thwarted if America used its intelligence services properly.

Russia: Vladimir Putin is a former KGB officer who understands how to wield power. That's been his entire life's work. He sees himself as the next Peter the Great and as someone who. Will reassemble the grandness of the Soviet Empire. He is hell bent to destroy NATO and demonstrate it to be an empty feckless vessel. He's well on his way with the invasions of Georgia, a massive hybrid war ongoing in Ukraine. You should look to him to provide some major provocations in the remaining time of the Obama Administration. He's restarting the Cold War in every way, even now building 40 new state of the art Mobile nuclear missiles, each carrying four warheads. Think of that, 160 American cities vulnerable to extinction from brand new weaponry. Putin has no real opposition and his propaganda goes not only unchecked but even unanswered by America and the west as the U.S. Govt has downsized or cancelled much of its VOA World service. People that live in oppressed areas really do listen, and they listen even harder when their host government tried to jam the signals. Putin can be managed but the full spectrum of statecraft must be unleashed on him. Russia is a far greater threat than China.

As one studies the continuum of options for a policy maker to respond on a national security or prevent a diplomatic incident, the options currently range from diplomats and press conferences "strenuously denouncing" some unwanted national behavior to quickly giving way to air strikes and predator drones. In the middle of this continuum there should exist a whole other tool kit of options to draw on long before uniformed soldiers and jet bombers arrive on scene. For the $80 billion spent on the intel community now we are missing that tool kit of Political and Surrogate warfare, covert action, sabotage, information war, propaganda etc. Yes those actions are difficult and come with risk but they are entirely indispensable at crucial junctions in a nations conduct. We are missing these dark arts now. Our Intel services are risk averse to the point of impotency. Many of the brush fires consuming the Middle East, Africa and SE Asia could have been solved by timely Covert Actions. Specific problems and solutions sets can be addressed in person.

Veterans Administration : The Federal Government has no business running health care systems. There are a reported still 600,000 and even up to 1,000,000 vets are still waiting for health care. An IG report found 300,000 deceased Vets still on the rosters for receiving care. Clearly government medicine is never going to get it done. Scrape the VA off and unleash the finest private healthcare system in the world. Vouchers work for broken public schools, use the same paradigm for our Wounded Vets. They can use a Tri-care like access (like any retired military veteran) for private healthcare. Privatize the VA hospitals and turn over their administration to some of the successful not for profit health care networks in America today. The easiest way to do this is to offer Vouchers for the Vets so they can opt out of a failing system. No one can criticize you for throwing the ones that are waiting an immediate lifeline. They will all end up opting out and the system will contract and fold as it should.

Thanks for your time.
I can be reached at

b6
b7C

Keep fighting.

From: steve bannon [ ]
To: corey r lewandowski
                [ ]; corey r. lewandowaski
                [ ]
Cc:
Bcc:
Subject: Talking Points.pdf
Date: Tue Sep 08 2015 04:07:00 EDT
Attachments: Talking Points.pdf.PDF

From   : Steve Bannon [ ]
Sent   : 9/8/2015 4:07:46 AM
To   : Corey R Lewandowski [ ]; Corey R. Lewandowaski
[ ]
Subject : Talking Points.pdf
Attachments : Talking Points.pdf

[ ] worked this up for u guys

From: Steve Bannon
Sent: Sat 9/12/2015 2:01 PM (GMT-04:00)
To: Corey Lewandowski
Cc:
Bcc:
Subject: Re: [redacted]

b6
b7C

Smart

Does DJT want a telephonic briefing from prince?...can set that up for 6pm today

From: Corey R Lewandowski <[redacted]>
Sent: Saturday, September 12, 2015 1:59:29 PM
To: Steve Bannon
Subject: Re: [redacted]

Yes. Good. We are meeting with Flynn on Monday

> On Sep 12, 2015, at 12:58 PM, Steve Bannon <[redacted]> wrote:
>
>
> Just got off the phone w/ him
>
> Did u get a chance to review his briefing memo?

From:
To: Steve Bannon
Cc:

Bcc:
Subject: Re: Breitbart News
Date: Sat Dec 12 2015 14:20:52 EST
Attachments:

Hey want to talk with you about the things we need to do regarding data collection

Thanks,

                    Breitbart News

Sent from my Verizon Wireless 4G LTE DROID

Steve Bannon   wrote:

        is our   and working on a story about the rubio/christie versus cruz/rand fight over NSA and the approval of the post-patriot act surveillance

From: Steve Bannon
To:

Cc:
Bcc:
Subject:
Date: Thu Jan 14 2016 19:59:07 EST
Attachments:

There is a guy I know very well currently living in india _____
_____ -smart guy _____ .. he is
muslim and could be a great asset to intel community

Do u have anybody in india who could meet w/ him and check him out

b6
b7C

From:	EP
To:	Steve Bannon
Cc:	
Bcc:	
Subject:	Re:
Date:	Thu Mar 17 2016 03:55:48 EDT
Attachments:	

Yes and yes!

Erik Prince

> On Mar 17, 2016, at 08:53, Steve Bannon <　　　　　　　> wrote:
>
> Can I get u on the show on monday???
>
> R u still up for meeting trump?

From: EP [redacted]
To: Steve Bannon [redacted]

Cc: [redacted]

Bcc:
Subject: Fwd: Recommended meeting
Date: Mon May 23 2016 15:04:44 EDT
Attachments: FullSizeRender.jpg

Resend with [redacted] included.

Erik Prince

Begin forwarded message:

From: EP [redacted]
Date: May 23, 2016 at 23:02:37 GMT+4
To: Steve Bannon [redacted]
Subject: Recommended meeting

Steve [redacted] Russia's actions in the Ukraine, the Middle East and their more aggressive posture of late are certainly issues that Mr Trump needs to understand fluently. Please consider meeting with Oleg to hear the perspective of a nation on the receiving end... He's the Nat Sec Adviser of Ukraine. He will be in DC from Tuesday to Friday this week.

Oleg is being escorted by my good friend [redacted] from LA. He's in the aerospace business.

Once you have any approvals needed we can sort the meeting logistics.

Best
Erik Prince

b6
b7C

b6
b7C

Hladkovskyy Oleg Vladimirovich
First Deputy Secretary of the National

Security and Defense Council of Ukraine

b6
b7C

From:	EP
To:	Steve Bannon
Cc:	
Bcc:	
Subject:	Russia/US election
Date:	Tue Oct 18 2016 19:30:00 EDT
Attachments:	

RUSSIAN ELECTION INFLUENCE ISSUE:

Mr. T should introduce an alternative narrative on the issue.   Consider this response:

It's unclear to me if Russia is directly involved in attempting to influence the US election.   That said, its safe to say they are keenly interested, and likely using surrogates to poke into the US election process.   Who does the Kremlin want to see in the White House? Ms. Clinton.   They know her well.   Putin and his Foreign Minister Lavarov are skilled interlocutors.   Professional, successful diplomat with some interesting postings in his career.   Was he a real foreign ministry officer or an intelligence officer serving under cover on his multiple tours?   The briefings I currently get don't provide this type of information.   Whatever his status, Mr. Lavarov has a first person assessment of Ms. Clinton.   He and Putin know her personality; they know her decision making processes.   They know her inner circle members, all their weaknesses and vulnerabilities.   They know Ms. Clinton's, personal and systemic weaknesses in the way she ran the State Department and how she responds to pressure and crisis. There is much to learn by analyzing Benghazi, Syria, Iraq and Iran policy development and implementation. All these major policy issues have failed to produce success or acceptable outcomes for the United States.   It has always been clear in person performance evaluations that the best predictor of future performance is past performance.   Ms. Clinton has a history of poor decision making, poor performance, and failure.   One could ask, who does the Kremlin prefer in this election? Its crystal clear to me. YOU Ms. Clinton, they know you, they know your weaknesses and your penchant for recklessness, ignoring rules and regulation which has provided a treasure trove of sensitive information while you were Secretary of State.   In phrase, You are predictable.   They prefer to deal with predictability and known deficiencies with a clear track record of bad decisions and failure.

I am largely an unknown.   Unknowns carry risk for our opponents.

Sent from my iPad

		b6
From:	Erik	b7C
To:	Steve Bannon	
Cc:		
Bcc:		
Subject:	Fwd: Bannon	
Date:	Wed Nov 16 2016 16:34:50 EST	
Attachments:		

We are getting you more PR help. FYI.

Begin forwarded message:

From: Mark Corallo

Date: November 16, 2016 at 22:32:52 GMT+1

To:

Subject: Fwd: Bannon

I spoke to her last night. Then she emailed this morning and I told her I was available. She still hasn't called back. But seen below that I sent to her.

Sent from my iPhone

Begin forwarded message:

From: Mark Corallo

Date: November 16, 2016 at 3:47:16 PM EST

To:

Subject: Bannon

This is the key to winning. This is who he is. This is the message every reporter who is doing a "profile" of Bannon should receive. They should be told that everything they need to know about him and his worldview is right here. It's fantastic.

And I'd suggest calling me at some point when you have a chance to discuss a great opportunity with VF which could happen tomorrow.

https://www.buzzfeed.com/lesterfeder/this-is-how-steve-bannon-sees-the-entire-world?utm_term=jqMQVJLMb#.ixGBQKgDA

And so he'll know he and I are of like mind, read this (and show it to him if you'd like).

http://www.nationalreview.com/article/226904/can-i-bailout-bailout-mark-corallo

Mark

Corallo Media Strategies

520 North Washington Street

Alexandria, VA 22314

703-838-9705

www.corallomediastrategies.com

From: Steve Bannon
Sent: Mon 6/08/2015 1:07 PM (GMT-04:00)
To: Steve Bannon
Cc:
Bcc:
Subject: Fw: Fwd: CONFIDENTIAL PROPOSAL
Attachments: CLINTON FOUNDATION BRIEFING AND EMAIL VECTOR PROPOSAL 05 17 2018.doc;
ATT00001.htm

From: [ ]

Sent: Friday, June 5, 2015 8:24:10 PM
To: Steve Bannon
Subject: Fwd: CONFIDENTIAL PROPOSAL
privileged and confidential

b6
b7C

Begin forwarded message:

From: Barbara Ledeen [ ]
Subject: **CONFIDENTIAL PROPOSAL**
Date: June 5, 2015 at 5:22:43 PM PDT
To: [ ]

Dear [ ]

Thank you for calling me so promptly. Here is the proposal. I hope we can finally work together!
Best-
Barbara

FBI(19cv1278)-322

SB_00018384

PROPOSAL FOR INVESTIGATIVE SERVICES

Executive Summary

This is a proposal for obtaining and then providing multi-level forensic analysis of the emails of certain accounts linked to the former Secretary or State, Hillary Clinton, as well as other members of the William, Hillary and Chelsea Clinton Foundation because of its known acceptance of foreign money from organizations, institutions, individuals and cut-outs of dubious distinction.

Hillary Clinton created a private domain server to host her personal email account, and this account was also used for Official U.S. Government business. It is the intent and spirit of the law that high level officials use only Government domains when conducting official business.

Preliminary research shows that millions of dollars were accepted by the Foundation at or around the time that the donors received a *quid pro quo* from the U.S. Government generally or the U.S. State Department specifically.

How the donations were characterized or washed before they landed at the Foundation in an effort to conceal the true owner is classic money laundering.

Key to any opposition research is to overlay advanced analytics performed by high-quality intelligence analysts using integrated visual analytic products that highlight connections, links, associations and relationships onto the databases: In other words to highlight that which is otherwise hidden in plain sight.

The issue is not whether data exists, but rather, sorting through the quantity of obtainable data and distilling from it the type of information that opposition research analysts use.

1

Opposition research also includes behavior and predictive profiling and it is highly dependent upon quality intelligence from a multiplicity of disparate database sources.

There is no email address within a private domain service (such as what Mrs. Clinton did here) or a public email domain service that cannot be penetrated using enough brute force intrusion or forensic tools. In the private sector, many tools exist that are legal and proper and often are capable of recovering seemingly deleted emails, but which are later found in the Deep Web, the Dark Web, the Peer-to-Peer and on private, but leaking domain servers of the recipients or re-senders.

Our view is that the private Clinton email domain server was, in all likelihood, breached long ago. The Chinese Intelligence Services, together with the Russian and Iranian cyber intelligence forces co-equally or alone could re-assemble the server's email content and easily transection it to contributions, lobby funds, travel records and the like, for Pres. Clinton and former Secretary Clinton.

From an operational security perspective alone, what Mrs. Clinton and her advisers did by creating a private email domain server displayed a level of recklessness that is unsurpassed by any Cabinet official in the history of email communications.

Our opinion is that before anyone touched the suspect emails, the server had to have been imaged by a highly qualified lab that the Clinton law firm would have carefully selected.

We opine that a time line study analysis would most likely show that the Clinton claims that the server was deleted after a thorough analysis of it was done, is not plausible, and therefore, untruthful.

Privileged and Confidential — Attorney Work Product

We opine that the entire email data mass from the Clinton private domain server does exist somewhere. Whether the content is in the hands of malevolent forces, such as certain foreign services, or whether they have benignly fallen into the Deep Web, the Dark Web, or Poor-to-Peer spheres remains to be seen.

We recommend: 1. That we search the open-source information sphere first, using the most advanced recovery tools in the marketplace, which our company does possess. Such a study can be done in less than 30 days. The cost would be approximately $22,000 and would be a worldwide search. 2. Next, we would see whether the content of the server fell into or was the subject of an attempted hacking event. It would take considerable study to see what could be recovered. The study would take 30-45 days and cost about $45,000. 3. We would check and see whether (a) the server was penetrated and recovered by specialized units within the Services and (b) the content of the server was transferred and (c) if any emails could be obtained. If even a single email were recovered and the providence of that email was a foreign service, it would prove catastrophic to the Clinton campaign and to the Foundation's work. This type of work requires travel and intermediary work. It would take 90-120 days, and cost somewhere between $290,000 to $350,000.

Summary and Overview

This is a proposal for providing multi-level forensic email study of certain accounts linked to the former Secretary of State, Hillary Clinton, as well as other members of the William, Hillary and Chelsea Clinton Foundation because of its known acceptance of foreign money from organizations, institutions, individuals and cut-outs of dubious distinction.

Preliminary research shows that millions of dollars were accepted by the Foundation at or around the time that the donors received a *quid pro quo* from United States Government generally or the U.S. State Department specifically.

Perhaps more egregious is how the donations were characterized or washed before they landed at the Foundation. Under normal circumstances, the re-classification and washing of funds in an effort to conceal the true owner is classic money laundering. This, combined with a number of other circumventions that the Clinton family is known to have engaged in during their 30 years in office, speaks volumes about the candidate's character and her willingness to live outside the boundaries of normal legalities.

Privileged and Confidential — Attorney Work Product

Methodology and Process

Because the Clinton Foundation as well as the Candidate have huge digital fingerprints, key to any opposition research is to overlay advanced analytics performed by high-quality intelligence analysts using integrated visual analytic products that highlight connections, links, associations and relationships onto the databases: In other words, to highlight that which is otherwise hidden in plain sight.

The issue is not whether data exists, but rather, sorting through the quantity of obtainable data and distilling from it the type of information that oppositional research analysts use.

While opposition research generally is defined as derogatory, negative, or adverse information it also includes behavior and predictive profiling. It is highly dependent upon quality intelligence from a multiplicity of disparate database sources.

Missing Email Recovery Project

Vast media reports show that Hillary Clinton created a private domain server to host her personal email account, and that this account was also used for Official US Government business. It is the intent and spirit of the law that high level officials use only Government domains when conducting official business.

There are a number of compelling reasons that such figures should never use a private email domain, to include Gmail, Hot Mail, Yahoo, etc. None accord the user absolute protection against intrusion by foreign intelligence services. In the main, there is no email address within a private domain service (such as what Mrs. Clinton did here) or a public email domain service that cannot be penetrated using enough brute force intrusion or forensic tools. In the private sector, many tools exist that are legal and proper and often are capable of recovering seemingly deleted emails, but which are later found in the Deep Web, the Dark Web, the Peer-to-Peer and on private, but leaking domain servers of the recipients or re-senders.

In the public sector, foreign intelligence services have a vast array of tools at their disposal that can penetrate any private email account, and many that are even U.S. Government protected systems.

The Clinton Foundation did not consider the upkeep and maintenance of a private email domain service, to include the most advanced firewalls, malwear, and resistant fortress sonic wall software that is available in the market place. Such upkeep must be done proactively and on a second-by-second basis, as new and even more aggressive viruses are created each and every second by malevolent forces around the world.

Our view is that the private Clinton email domain server was, in all likelihood breached long ago. One of the dangers of handing over the entire server to an independent forensic data scientist is that the residue of such a breach could be found and highlighted and in some cases, even traced back to the offender. Such a report over a breach of this type would be political suicide for the former Secretary of State, who held one of the most sensitive positions in the US Government.

Second, the Chinese Intelligence Services, together with the Russia and Iranian Cyber Intelligence Forces co-equally or alone could re-assemble the server's email content and easily transcction it to contributions, lobbying funds, travel records, and the like for President Clinton

4

Privileged and Confidential – Attorney Work Product –

and former Secretary Clinton. In short, they could do what the U.S. conservative media and its supporters are trying to do today. However, they would have two distinct advantages that nobody in the private media enjoy:

a. They would have the emails, both the originals, headers, footers, attachments, and the communication vectors of the benefactors seeking patronage with the Clintons and the Foundation. All of this would be in original, pristine, and undeleted condition for them to cross section against open source data.

b. The Services would also have not only extremely experienced HUMINT analysts, but advanced analytical software that could transection contribution of dollars against emails and their timing; as well as other disparate data to assemble a mosaic of political pay-to-play story. The Services could then seek to blackmail members of the Foundation, its staff, or even the Clinton's themselves. If they did not cooperate, the Services could selectively leak pieces of their analytic findings such as what was done on the Russian uranium story.

Thus, from an operational security perspective alone, what Mrs. Clinton and her advisors did by creating a private email domain server displayed a level of recklessness that is unsurpassed by any Cabinet official in the history of email communications.

Deletion of Email Server Content -- Implausibility

One of the issues that has not been well-briefed in the media is the forensic methodology of email deletion and recovery, making the story behind what the Clinton Foundation and Mrs. Clinton specifically, a total fantasy.

First, when an email domain server has content that is going to be "parsed" for deletion of select data, such as personal emails versus government business email it must be done in a very precise and logical manner.

No expert would ever, under any circumstances whatsoever, work with the virgin or original source email server. Any reputable forensic expert would make an "image copy" of the domain server first, and moreover, do a sector-by-sector image copy (the most invidious and thorough method possible) and work from the image to do qualitative or quantitative deletion of the "unneeded emails". Nobody would ever risk the potential of the original content server being corrupted, accidentally deleted, or suffer some sort of catastrophic failure[1] because it would be devastating politically to try and "message" that kind of event.

Thus, our opinion is that Williams and Connolly would hire a reputable forensic shop which would advise that the domain server to be examined for specific content be imaged, and at least once.

Second, it is not plausible that a human decision-making process was used to manually review every single email, either on the server (or an image of the server) and cull out only those that were non-personal. It is implausible as to the amount of time such an endeavor would take, as well as the thoroughness of such a process. According to media reports, the suspect server had

---

[1] Not to reference history, but the modern day version of the Rose Mary Wood 18 minute tape gap that occurred upon the infamous Watergate Tapes episode, made more implausible by the forensically enhanced sound engineers who showed repeated re-deletes of the same tape sectors

Privileged and Confidential -- Attorney Work Product --

SB_00018389
FBI(19cv1278)-327

approximately 60,000 emails, of which approximately 32,000 were allegedly personal and were deleted.

It is not clear how this was done, according to these same media reports. Logically, there are only three ways:

a. **Review, print and decide.** The first method is for a human analyst to sit and review each email manually on a computer that had been loaded with the .ost or .pst file that contained the email. For those that were "business", the analyst printed a copy in paper format and laid the email on the side. For those emails that had attachments, this too would be printed and attached to the printed email. However, one must consider the human and mechanical time elements to go through 60,000 emails in order to complete such a task, and do it using only one machine, one printer, and one analyst.[2]

b. **Key Word Searching.** Here again, assuming that the legal team prohibited an image copy, the analyst would go through the .pst with inherently loaded key word searching software (and this assumes such software was natively on the domain email server to accomplish such a task) and formulate the compliant search terms to distinguish what was or was not a US Government business email.

Some possible key words would be domain server extensions that would be commonly used by US Government personnel, such as .mil, .gov, .State etc. However, even key word searching to try and cull out the potential government emails from the total data mass would not be a definitive solution. Moreover, to go through thousands of potential hits and cull out only those that would be relevant by a single analyst (Again, hypothetically, no image copy was done) would take an enormous amount of time.

c. **Load COTS analytic or key word software.** No forensic analyst would risk loading any type of software onto the native machine or domain server in an effort to identify possible relevant emails.

Most likely, they would image the domain server, and then load the COTS software onto the machine and see whether it could be configured to work with the Clinton domain server. Domain servers and operating systems all have their own unique idiosyncrasies which must be accommodated when selecting a particular COTS software to do email recovery based on key words.

For example, the leading COTS email key word recovery software for Microsoft Outlook email was **XOBNI** (it was developed and engineered by the creators and original coders of MS-Outlook and later sold to Yahoo) but trying to load this product or its Yahoo successor equivalent onto certain domain servers can cause not only a crash, but destruction of files. The reason is that all email key word search tool products require "indexing" of the entire mass to be successful.[3]

---

[2] As stated, this hypothetical scenario assumes that the original was not imaged, and therefore only one person could work on the file at a time.

[3] "Indexing" by its very nature means to pulverize the .pst, .ost or equivalent file on the domain server, and then to parse it in such a way so that the searcher can type into the program a key word, date, time, reference, citation, or Boolean-logic scripted term and bring back a result which would contain the framed "phrase". "Indexing" is inherently a very complex data process that can damage a file if done by a program that does not accommodate different operating systems.

6

Privileged and Confidential — Attorney Work Product

Confidential — Confidential Treatment Requested

Whether Google Desk Top or other popular COTS programs, the data mass involved must be completely indexed, front-to-back. Depending on the type of operating system within the Clinton domain server, and moreover, the kinds of emails and attachments from around the world that she was sending and receiving, defines how well the indexing will work, and moreover, whether it will damage or destroy the native, original file.

For all of these and other technical and esoteric reasons, logic and normal forensic methodology demands that before anyone touched the suspect emails, the server had to have been imaged and done by a highly qualified lab that the Clinton law firm (David Kendall, Esq., and Williams and Connolly) would have carefully selected.

Assuming our hypothetical -- that at least one image was done -- next would be the process used to select, segregate, and decide what to do with each of over 60,000 emails over a compressed period of time.

One of the issues that the media has overlooked is the forensic process for "decisioning" emails for segregation and the amount of time it would take to cull out of a data mass select emails of relevance within 60,000 emails.

For these reasons, the customer here needs to create a plausibility time line to show the Clinton claims unfeasible. To create such a time line, certain assumptions need to be evaluated or at a minimum, made. For example:

1. When was the domain server created?
2. What was the last date in which it was used?
3. When was it shut down and no longer capable of sending or receiving traffic?
4. When was the domain server deemed a "problem" that legal counsel had to consider?
5. When could the domain server been removed from the Clinton residence or wherever it was being hosted and then moved to either Williams and Connolly offices in Washington, or to the lab that they elected.
6. When did the first emails that were considered US Government trickle over to the State Department or some other agency to be considered for release?

The point here is that to process, decision, and output 60,000 emails, we speculate that it could not have been done in a matter of weeks or even months. To prove our assumption, one need only do a time study analysis (TSA) upon those emails that were produced (those that the customer currently does possess or have access to) and conduct an alpha-omega study of how long such emails as contained in a like domain server would take to identify, isolate, read, analyze, decision, print, and stack -- and do all of this on a single non-imaged hard drive that purports to be the original content server; and be done by a single human analyst.

At the end of the day, we opine that such a time line study analysis would most likely show that the Clinton claims that the server was deleted after a thorough analysis of it was done is not plausible and therefore, untruthful.

Recovery of Emails Deleted From Third Party Sources

We opine that the entire email data mass from the Clinton private domain server does exist somewhere. Whether the content is in the hands of malevolent forces, such as certain foreign services, or whether they have benignly fallen into the Deep Web, Dark Web, or Peer-to-Peer spheres remains to be seen.

7

Privileged and Confidential -- Attorney Work Product --

Multi-Phase Email Recovery Approach

1. We recommend that the customer start with a search of the open source sphere first, using the most advanced recovery tools in the marketplace, which our company does possess and can do. The critical search term is the email server MX codes, the headers or footers of the email server, or at a minimum, the domain server name which is fairly unique.

   Such as study could be done in less than 30 days, the cost would be approximately $22,000 and would be a worldwide search. For this small amount, if we are lucky and the tools used are able to troll the open source sphere well, we could actually bring back the content of sent or received emails.

2. Next, it is possible that through intermediary sources and methods, we could try and see whether the content of the server fell into or was the subject of an attempted hacking event. To do this, we would need to do a careful study of the domain server residue that can be recovered via open source sources as the forensic structure of the domain server as it last existed, would still be in the Internet sphere, but would take considerable study to see what could be recovered. The study would take 30 to 45 days and cost about $45,000.00

3. Finally, we could check with our own HUMINT sources that have access through liaison work with various foreign services and see whether (a) the server was penetrated and recovered by specialized units within the Services (b) the content of the server was transferred and (c) if any emails could be obtained. Even if a single email was recovered and the providence of that email was a foreign service, it would prove catastrophic to the Clinton campaign and moreover, to the Foundation's work. However, to do this type of work, much travel and intermediary work is needed. It would take about 90 to 120 days, cost somewhere between $290,000 to $350,000.

Clinton Foundation Proposal
Introduction and Overview

The Clinton Foundation, the organization that the client seeks to obtain specific information upon, would involve significant research using both public, private, proprietary and restricted access database systems that we are licensed to subscribe to. At present, many media experts are trolling sources and working this landscape furiously. What is missing is the key determinator and that is the email contents and the date of each. These, transected against the Clinton Foundation contributors defines whether this was a pay-to-play organization.

There is historical precedence in Presidential campaigns using nefarious devices and vehicles to accord benefactors' opportunity to "pay and play". Indeed, Hilary Clinton herself was intimately involved in this.

Some initial tests of the data sources that we need to access revealed that it is complex searching, requiring professionals who have substantial experience in different kinds of sophisticated search methodology, not normally done by generalists.

Task 1 – Foundation Project

1. Conduct a full financial on the Foundation that would include accessing all banking accounts, assets, credit, financial holdings and investments (domestic & overseas) of the Subject. Determine funds deposited and identify names of foreign and domestic donors from 2009 to the present.

Task 2 – Foundation Project

1. Determine whether subject may have any hidden interests in the companies or persons directly or through proxies or through other arms distance donors.

2. Identify Subject's "Top 10 Donors" list and obtain searchable terms, (known as "the entity" or "entities") to include names of people associated with cited companies; or names of companies associated with cited names, and then run those names, addresses, and other identifiers against both State and Federal Campaign records, as well as published and non-published Political Action Committee

3. Identify the names of contributors, their addresses, and telephone numbers and compare against a database of successful contracts and attempted bids filed in the State Department between 2009-2013.

4. Determine any personal dealings (quid pro quo) between the subject and the top donors between 2009-2013.

5. International or other unusual financial activities including political donations. Confirm that the subject has previously disclosed all international financial transactions or donations that might be construed as international in sourcing. If international transactions exist, we will identify them and recommend potential secondary courses of action including, but limited to, identification of the sources.

Costs

The searches for the Foundation study are costly owing to the fact that the funds of interest came from outside of the United States, and therefore international resources must be used to gain access to the needed accounts that were used to send funds. The initial feasibility study to see what the weight and amount of data that exists is $24,900. The probably cost to do a full search, assuming that we can document the claims made by the current sources probably will range somewhere between $230,000 and $300,000.

Personal Background Searches -- How Data Is Catalogued and Accessed

The customer may also be interested in doing our GlobalScan searches, which are the deepest, and most in-depth scans that are available in the commercial database world today. Reports can range from 800 to 4000 pages long, when including exhibits. Our GlobalScans can be done on any person in the world, and costs depend on the name, address, age and other identifiers for the person. To date, our firm has processed over 20,000 GlobalScans since our inception in 1978. After 1996, the GlobalScan always included digital media data, usually from the original source so that they could be used in a legal proceeding.

In real terms, every person today has a data fingerprint, much like their own fingerprint. As they operate in the e-commerce world, the "Data DNA" of their digital fingerprint leaves an indelible mark that is rarely able to be deleted. Spending patterns, financial transactions, telephone call pattern analysis, credit card transactions, travel habits, subscriptions to magazines and online computer behavior cannot be altered. While people often try to conceal or obfuscate their tracks, computer forensics can be employed to detect their connection.

Humans today translate into digital images, both structured and unstructured. Whether data, pictures, sounds, cyber visits -- all of it compose a person's data DNA that is unique to that person. It looks something like the illustration below:

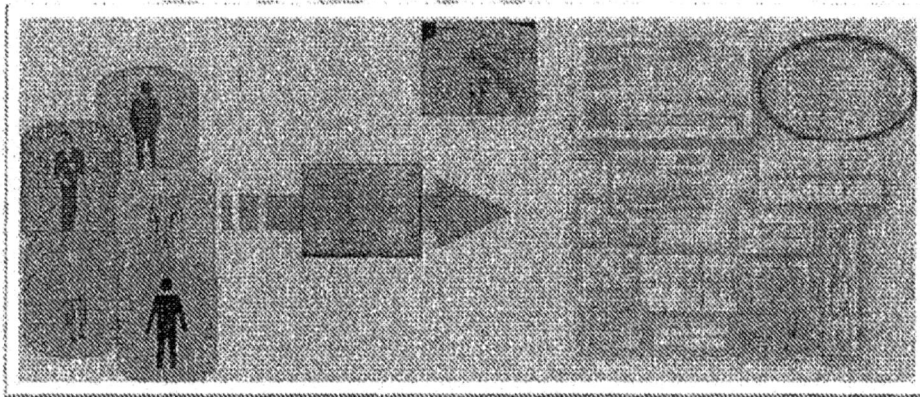

Advanced analytics are used to do data extraction, recognizing that:

- **80% of the world's digital content is *unstructured* or *semi-structured*, to include:**
  - Newspapers data sources
  - Financial statements contained deep within web sites

10

- o Government reports that are both open and closed
- o Press releases on the surface Web
- o Websites, both open and closed
- o Emails that are dumped into the public domain

◆ **Semantic extraction is typically used to**

- o Discover entities and identify their structural ownership and links
- o Discover relationships between entities
- o Discover events
- o Taxonomy generation
- o Categorize documents

◆ **A high-performance data-extraction system that consists of**

- o A design-time *compiler*
- o A run-time *engine*
- o A powerful *Integrated Development Environment (IDE)*
- o Several utility programs

◆ **Semantic extraction is typically used to**

- o Discover entities
- o Discover relationships between entities
- o Discover events
- o Categorize documents

Technically, entity extraction operates somewhat in this manner:

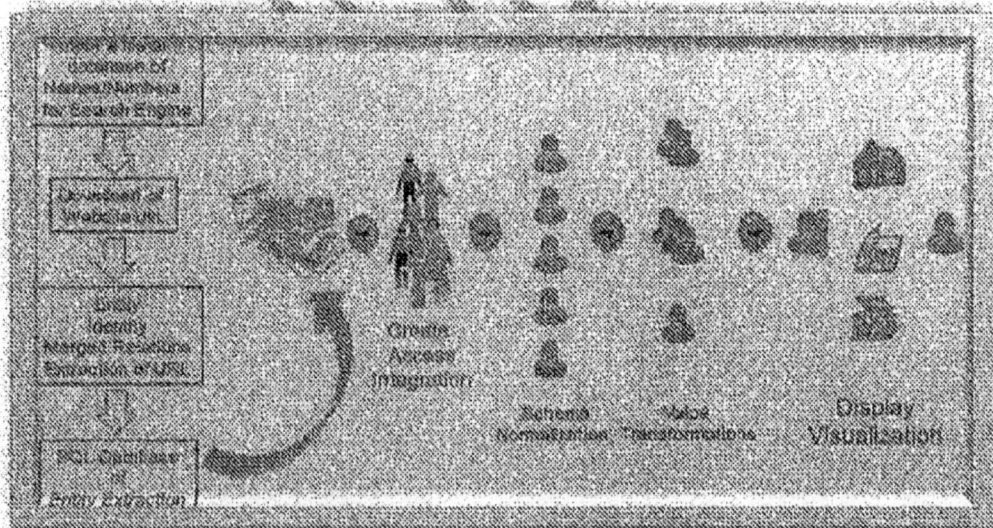

As stated at the outset, this investigation should be a phased inquiry, starting with the Global Scan® first, and once the results are obtained, we can probe the leads deeper and trace back related information, if any, to the original source.

ICI specializes in complex investigations that involve databases and electronic sources. It is our experience that the only effective way to conduct such a study is to conduct a Global Scan® on each person or company under investigation.

We assume permissible purpose exists for conducting all appropriate database searches. This matter is confidential and privileged and done pursuant to the privileged communications doctrine and the attorney work-product doctrine. Typically, Investigative Consultants is engaged through a client's law firm.

For further information regarding compliance with our Terms of Engagement, please see our web site at http: www.icioffshore.com[4]

Normally, all searches start with a basic scan of our systems, which we define as a *Global Scan®*. This search permits us to cite the costs for obtaining all other information within each "information corridor" that may be identified during the initial scan.

It also enables the ultimate client to maintain control of the scope, direction, and cost of a more extensive investigation. Each proposed search item is listed at the end of initial report.

For example, a Global Scan® will cite the name and address of a bank, an account number, the signatures on the account, and when it was opened, but will not provide information regarding balances or activity. However, the Global Scan® will cite the exact cost for obtaining that next level of information.

Normally, GlobalScan® always includes the following categories of data:

1. Banking, financial and credit relationships, including addresses and names of institutions.

2. Real estate holdings, real estate trusts, and real property conveyances.

3. Corporate affiliations, executive associations, and self-confessed employment.

4. Credit reports and personal financial scans.

5. Litigation, including criminal arrests in their areas of residence.

6. Newspaper, magazine, trade journal, and wire service reports.

---

[4] Please note that some searches require a permissible purpose as defined under the Federal Fair Credit Reporting Act, Title 15, USC 1681, et. seq., as well as other local, state, federal and international laws. You are required to certify to ICI that any search is in compliance with both FCRA, as well as the 1999 Graham-Leach Bank Privacy Act. By placing any order with ICI, the client represents that the client has fully complied with all local, state, federal and international laws and assumes all responsibility. ICI assumes no responsibility for determining whether the client is in compliance with these laws.

We are not a Consumer Credit Reporting Agency and all of our reports are done as an agent to counsel under the Attorney Work Product Doctrine. For further information, please see our Terms and Conditions, found at http://www.icioffshore.com/terms.html , which are incorporated into this proposal by reference.

12

Privileged and Confidential — Attorney Work Product

7. Known associates, family members and close personal friends who may be used to transfer or convey assets.

8. Vehicles, boats, mechanized equipment, and recreational devices traced to merchant's name, address or SSN.

9. UCC filings recorded in the name of the merchant, based upon a scan of the person's name, SSN, or past addresses, a triple secured search. Included is both debtor and secured party searches.

10. Identification of trade creditors, credit card companies, utility companies, banks, or other entities that the target would be paying with some type of instrument. These searches do not include identification of the bank that a check is drawn upon, or the account number, just the bill that is being paid.

11. Identification of telephone numbers, cellular numbers, and mobile telephone numbers; together with long distance carriers. This search does not include a detail of the numbers dialed, or the subscribers to the numbers dialed, which can only be obtained at the next level of searching.

12. All past addresses, historic use of addresses, names of relatives, names of persons traced to addresses used by the merchant, names of relatives and the statistical identifiers of those that reside in the same household as the merchant.

In actuality, the data flow appears something like that which is depicted below:

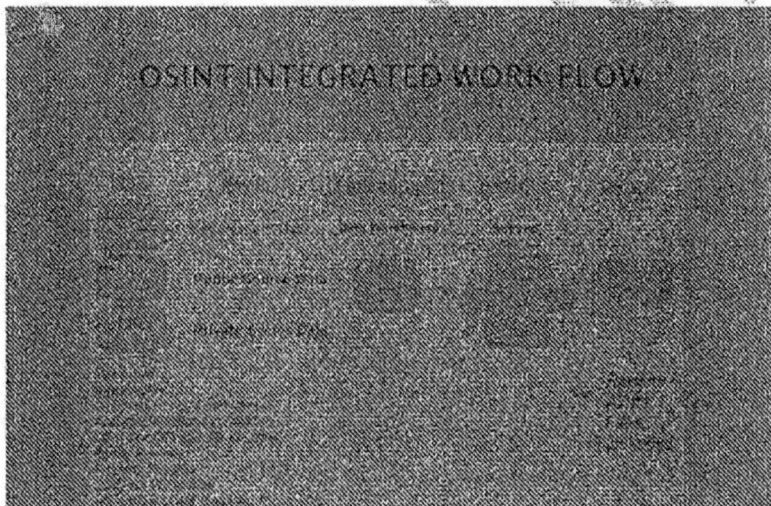

OSINT INTEGRATED WORK FLOW

Global Scan® is conducted on a flat fee basis only, and is marketed that way because clients seek to have a guaranteed fee structure cited in advance. Moreover, before any Global Scan® can be prepared, ICI requires that all cited fees and expense surcharges be paid in advance.

ICI does not bill by the hour for its services nor use "general price lists". Rather, it uses the "bundled billing" approach. In short, the fee is guaranteed and includes all research time, computer data downloads, analysis, report preparation and delivery. We may consult with counsel by telephone or email following transmission of our report, should there be a need to

Privileged and Confidential – Attorney Work Product

SB_00018397

FBI(19cv1278)-335

clarify a few points in our report. This approach guarantees the client all available information for a pre-cited charge without regard to the amount of information obtained.

Specialized In-Depth Searches

ICI also can conduct deeper probes, depending on the requirements of counsel, the permissible purpose to obtain the information, etc. In addition to the above mentioned eight categories of data, ICI can, under certain circumstances provide a more in-depth report and other kinds of advanced searching. The cost for each depends on the nature of the request. Some of the in-depth scans include:

1. Social Security Numbers and DOB Search;

2. Social Security Trace for all addresses, verify date of issuance, state of issuance and whether used regarding banking, financial or credit transaction;

3. Date of Birth Records;

4. Death Records;

5. Change Of Name Records;

6. Marriage and divorce Records;

7. Criminal Records State or federal sealed or unsealed felony or misdemeanor;

8. Warrants of Arrest;

9. Order of Protection, domestic violence offender scans;

10. Probation Records, special offender searches, including sex offender registries, or habitual offender status;

11. Property Tax Records;

12. Utility Bill Records;

13. Current Address;

14. Drivers License Information;

15. Car Insurance Records;

16. U.S. Postal Service Forwarding Address Records;

17. True owner of U.S. Postal Service PO BOX Records;

18. Magazines or Newsletters that you are the owner of. (Postal Records);

19. Bulk Mail Permit records (US Postal Service);

20. Magazines that someone may subscribe to;

21. Books that are obtained from a library;

22. Junk Mail/Catalogs register;

23. Credit Card Records;

24. Credit Records;

25. Banking, financial and credit relationships that include name and address of bank;

26. MVR Reports;

14

Privileged and Confidential — Attorney Work Product

27. TAG & VIN Traces;

28. License Plates (Name and address can be found by doing a license plate search:

29. Full Driving Records, including searches of National Major Offender Database;

30. Military Records Search, including discharge status, branch job and rating, dates of Enlistment, Reasons for Discharge;

31. List of Hospital admissions and possible diagnosis codes;

32. Telephone Number Historical Index ;

33. Cell Phone Trace;

34. Unlisted Phone Numbers Decodes;

35. Illegal Alien Database Scan;

36. Government Job Registration Scan:

37. Worker's Compensation Settlement or Claim Scans;

38. Automobile and Personal Injury Insurance Fraud Database;

39. Real Estate, Co-Op and Full Title Search scan for 50 years;

40. Leads for identifying hidden or secreted assets that are in the form of t-bills, bonds, stocks, "offshore" bank accounts, or funds in tax haven countries;

41. College Records Search, verification of college attendance, degrees conveyed and special awards;

42. Terrorist or Cult Member Dossiers;

43. Professional Certification by various professional trade associations;

44. Business Conduct Searches through databases such as Better Business Bureau;

45. Federal Bankruptcy Database Scans, including whether cited in an adversarial proceeding, or as a claimant in any bankruptcy action by others;

46. Catalogs, Mailing Lists, and Department Store searches;

47. Employment Searches for a period of 20 years, including job titles and descriptions, addresses, and possible level of compensation;

48. All Professional Licenses Scan;

49. Business licenses, motor vehicle licenses, pilot licenses;

50. Evictions and Tenant Landlord Database Scan;

51. Voter Registration Database and scan of historic voting record;

52. Email tracing service and complete Web Site Domain.

Worldwide Deep Web Intelligence Scan

By way of background, the "Deep Web" — a vast reservoir of Internet content that is 500 times larger than known "surface" World Wide Web material. What makes the discovery of the Deep Web so significant is the quality of content found within it. Deep Web searches are intended for cases where historic data (more than four years) needs to be obtained and which otherwise tends to "fall off" current-day data tables.

15

Searching on the Internet today can be compared to dragging a net across the surface of the ocean. While much can be gathered from the top, there is a wealth of information that lies deeper, and therefore is missed by the average person.

There are hundreds of billions of highly valuable documents hidden in searchable databases that cannot be retrieved by conventional search engines. The reason is simple: basic search methodology and technology has not evolved significantly since the inception of the Internet.

Traditional search engines create their card catalogs by spidering or crawling "surface" Web pages. To be identified, a page must be static and linked to subsequent other pages. Utilized in this manner, standard search engines cannot "see" or retrieve content in the Deep Web and the crawlers used by them cannot probe beneath the surface. The result is that enormous amounts of data remains untapped and effectively "hidden" to the crawler, while in reality, the material is in plain sight.

The discovery of the Deep Web is the result of groundbreaking search technology developed by the Intelligence Community. Private companies have only recently developed search technology capable of identifying, retrieving, qualifying, classifying and organizing "deep" and "surface" content from the World Wide Web.

The Deep Web is qualitatively different from the surface Web. Deep Web sources store their content in searchable databases that only produce results dynamically in response to a direct request. But a direct query is a "one at a time" laborious way to search.

Our search system automates the process of making dozens of direct queries simultaneously using multiple thread technology. It allows searchers to dive deep and explore hidden data simultaneously from multiple sources using directed queries.

Businesses, researchers and consumers now have access to the most valuable and hard-to-find information on the Web and can retrieve it with pinpoint accuracy. If the most coveted commodity of the Information Age is indeed information, then the value of Deep Web content is immeasurable.

When conducting Deep Web intelligence studies on companies or individuals, we access a much different class of documents. Included in the search results are not only the standard information retrieved by conventional search engines but many other possible leads. Some of the highlights of the Deep Web search include:

1. Public information on the Deep Web that is 400 to 550 times larger than the commonly defined World Wide Web;

2. 7,500 terabytes of information, compared to 19 terabytes of information in the surface Web;

3. 550 billion individual documents compared to the 1 billion of the surface Web;

4. Information from an additional 100,000 Deep Web sites;

5. 60 of the largest Deep Web sites collectively contain about 750 terabytes of information — sufficient by themselves to exceed the size of the surface Web by 40 times;

6. On average, Deep Web sites receive about 50% greater monthly traffic than surface sites and are more highly linked to than surface sites; however, the typical (median) Deep Web site is not well known to the Internet search public;

7. The Deep Web is the largest growing category of new information on the Internet;

8. Deep Web sites tend to be narrower with deeper content than conventional surface sites;

9. Total quality content of the deep Web is at least 1,000 to 2,000 times greater than that of the surface Web;

10. Deep Web content is highly relevant to every information need, market and domain. More than half of the deep Web content resides in topic specific databases;

11. A full 95% of the deep Web is publicly accessible information — not subject to fees or subscriptions.

To put these numbers in perspective, we estimate that some of the largest search engines, such as Northern Light, individually index only 16% of the surface Web. Since they are missing the Deep Web, Internet searchers are therefore searching only 0.03% — or one in 3,000 — of the content available to them today.

Clearly, simultaneous searching of multiple surface and Deep Web sources is necessary when comprehensive information retrieval is needed.

We have automated the identification of Deep Web sites and the retrieval process for simultaneous searches. We have also developed a direct-access query engine translatable to about 20,000 sites, already collected, eventually growing to 100,000 sites.
Our experience has shown that when the hit scores fall below 65%, they are not deemed reliable and the hits tend to be unrelated to the target of the inquiry.

Graphically, size comparison of the Deep Web compared to the "surface web" looks something like this:

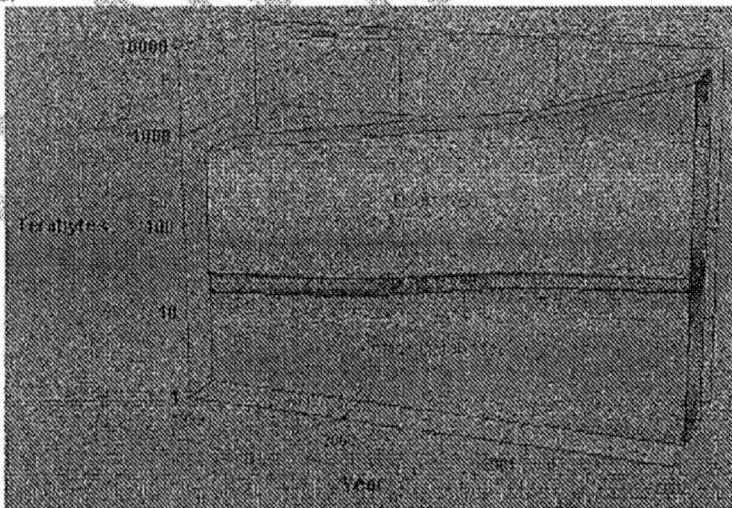

Dark Space Searching

During the past several years, the Department of Defense, led by the Defense Advanced Research Projects Agency (DARPA) has been steadily working on a project called the NOISE database, known as Name Only Index Searching and Exception. The acronym NOISE came from the negative consequence of conventional searching of the Open Source, Web-enabled applications such as:

www.altavista.com
www.northernlight.com
www.lycos.com
www.opendirectory.com
www.waybackmachine.org
www.google.com
www.euil.com
www.msn.com

Visually, the process of gathering information on a person or entity looks something like the figure below:

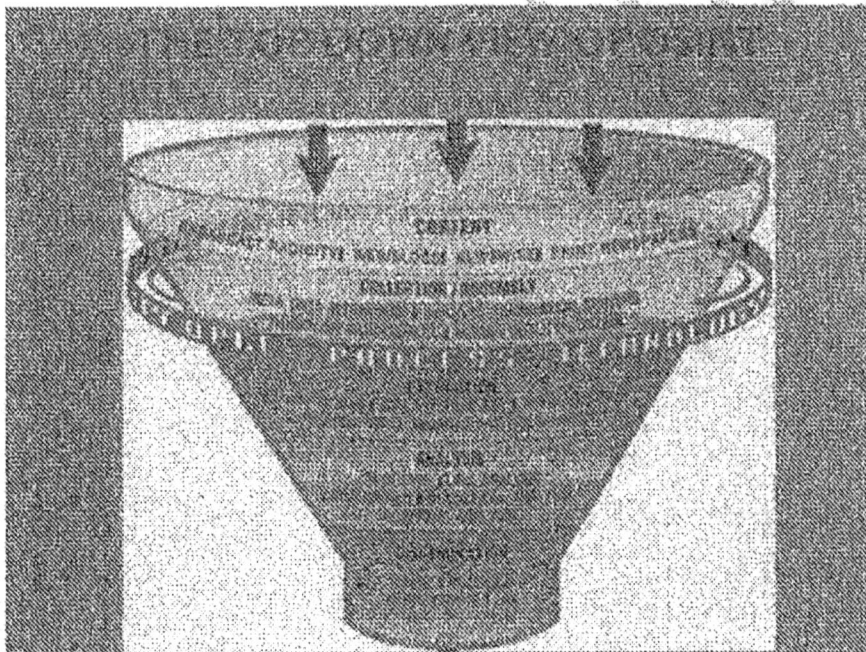

Privileged and Confidential — Attorney Work Product —

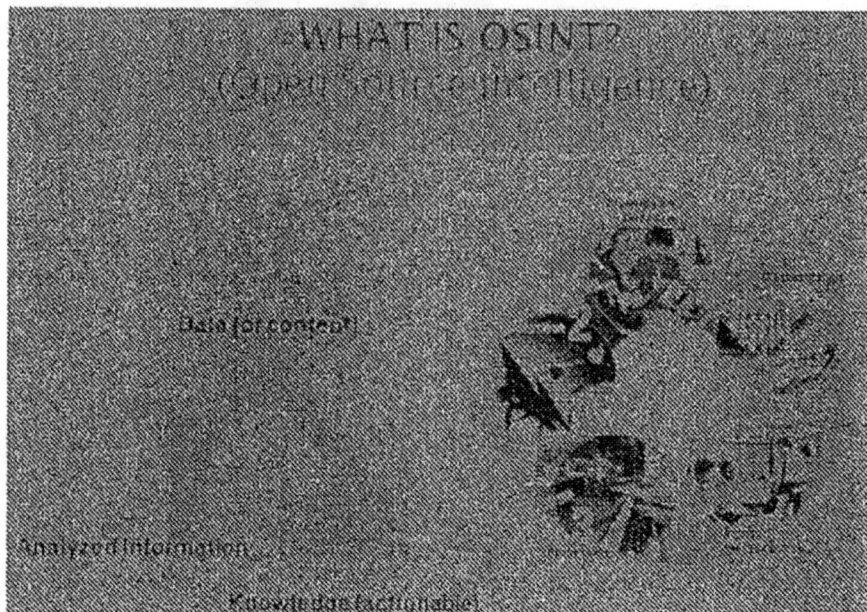

WHAT IS OSINT?
(Open Source Intelligence)

Data (or content)

Analyzed Information

Knowledge (actionable)

Traditionally, these are "Name Only" or "Business Name only" or "Telephone Number Only" searches that return massive, unrefined results. When the search criteria is common, the return results is often "NOISE" and burdens the analyst with a vast amount of irrelevant information.

In the commercial or legal markets space, the same is true, but the pressure is even greater to obtain results quickly, efficiently, and within a reasonable budget.

The commercial version of the NOISE application is particularly useful in Hedge Fund Defense Litigation and has been used by ICI on numerous occasions to "walk back" information claimed to be gleaned from "insiders", when in reality, it was fished out of the Deep Web and effectively converted for use by Hedge Fund analysts.

For that reason, we suggest that NOISE application and the IdentiChek® data searches be considered here because of the relatively common names of Advantage and the key individuals.

It is the union of the NOISE application and the restricted access data within IdentiChek® that is only available with a permissible purpose that allows for a highly relevant, targeted search approach. It looks something like this:

Privileged and Confidential – Attorney Work Product –

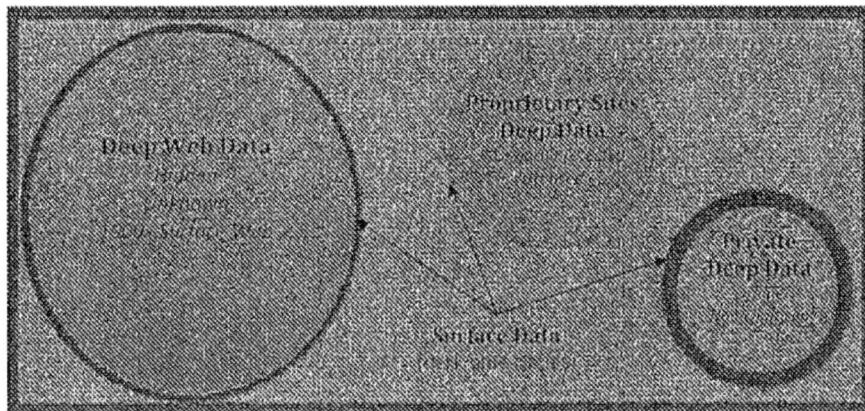

In the DoD contracting space, DARPA was tasked with the order to find a means to take granular data about a person (All known names, dates of birth, ages, past addresses, phone numbers, faxes, email addresses, web site addresses, businesses, names of relatives, etc.) or the so called digital fingerprint of a person, and inject that intelligence into the web-enabled application for a more definitive results.

For common names, the leads are culled down from perhaps 12,000 to 120. Moreover, the data is highly accurate and is considered rifle-shot searching.

The second compelling reason this new form of search technology was developed is that the Internet and the Deep Web is much larger and vaster than any database source on the planet today. The "Deep Web", sometimes known as the Internet Dark Space or the Deep Web Intelligence Center, is a vast reservoir of content that is 1,000 times larger than the known "surface" World Wide Web. What makes the discovery of the Deep Web so significant is the quality of content found within.

In a very real way, the Dark Space of the Internet is much like the outer space: Its depth and size is not measureable, indefinable, and endless.

The old way of searching, looks something like this:

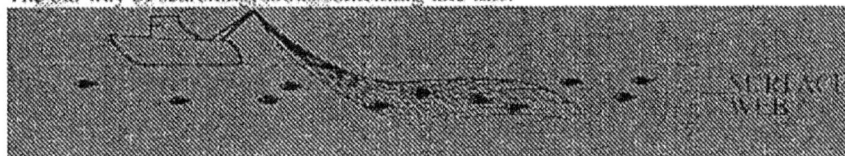

However, the new way, including use of NOISE and ICI IdentiChek data that can be granularized, looks something like this:

Privileged and Confidential — Attorney Work Product —

SB_00018404

FBI(19cv1278)-342

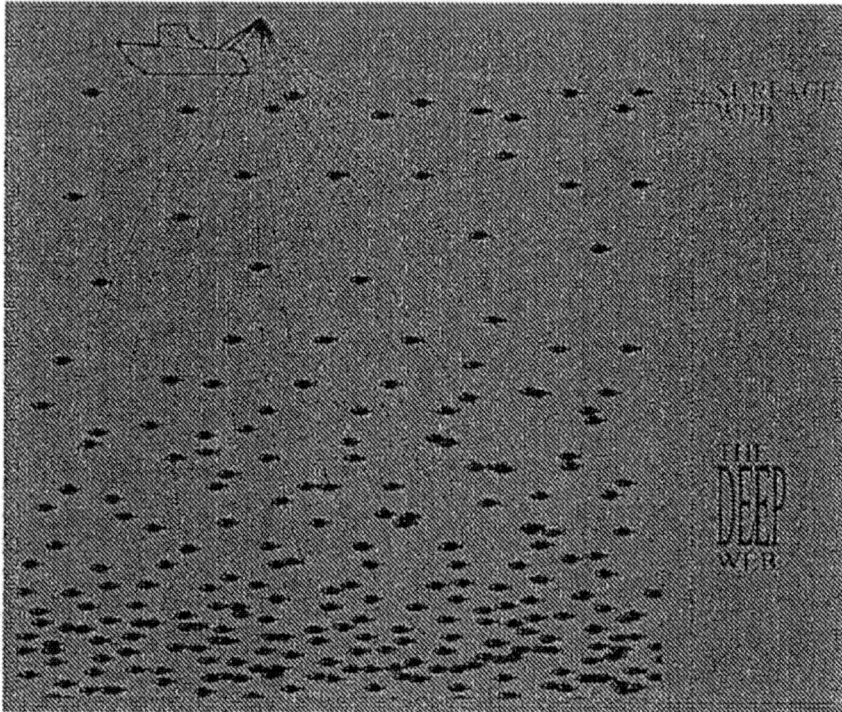

This new capability allows searchers to dive deep and explore hidden data from multiple sources simultaneously using directed queries.

When you combine the tools of being able to "Deep Dive" into the Internet, with the ability to access restricted and protected personal data that is mostly available only to law firms or those with a permissible purpose (Name, DOB, Past Addresses, etc.), one can significantly expand not only the searchable data mass, but do so with highly accurate results.

Businesses, researchers and consumers now have access to the most valuable and hard-to-find information on the Web and can retrieve it with pinpoint accuracy. Searching on the Internet today can be compared to dragging a net across the surface of the ocean.

However, there is a wealth of information that is deep, and therefore missed, hence, the Deep Web. The reason is simple: basic search methodology and technology have not evolved significantly since the inception of the Internet. Traditional search engines create their card catalogs by spidering or crawling "surface" Web pages.

To be discovered, the page must be static and linked to other pages. Traditional search engines cannot "see" or retrieve content in the Deep Web. Because traditional search engine crawlers cannot probe beneath the surface, the Deep Web or Dark Space of the Internet has heretofore been hidden in plain sight.

The Deep Web is qualitatively different from the surface Web. Deep Web sources store their content in searchable databases that only produce results dynamically in response to a direct request. But a direct query is a "one at a time" laborious way to search.

21

SB_00018405

FBI(19cv1278)-343

NOISE automates the process of making dozens of direct queries simultaneously using multiple thread technology, and takes private, non-public financial information and pulverizes it for inclusion into the search query. If the most coveted commodity of the Information Age is indeed intelligence, then the value of Deep Web content is immeasurable.

Today, more and more people are "self-confessing" their habits and haunts; their biases and prejudices and their flavors and peccadillos. It is most predominantly done on such Social Media web sites as Facebook, MyLife, LinkedIn, and hundreds of other public and private chat portals. All of these locations are trawled, but the key is the search instrument or vehicle used and the advanced analytics applies.

ICI specializes in the developing of these wide and deep data mining nets and tools, where it is launched upon an endlessly sized ocean of data.

Some of these data sources include:

Privileged and Confidential – Attorney Work Product –

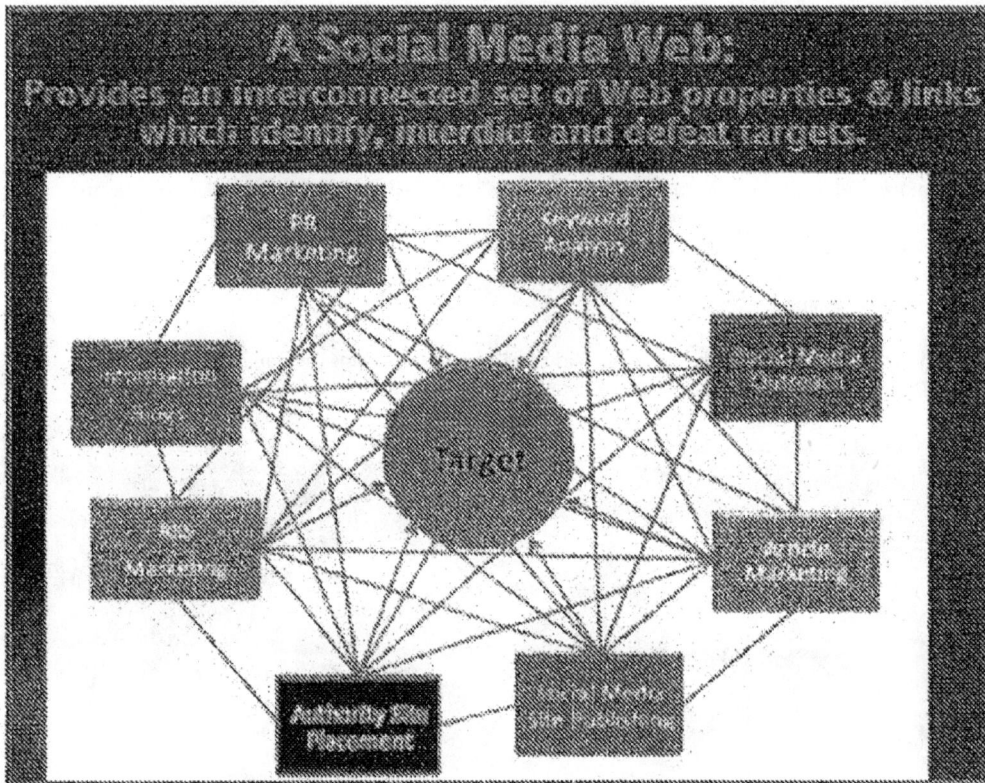

A Social Media Web:
Provides an interconnected set of Web properties & links which identify, interdict and defeat targets.

History of ICI's Products and Services

Investigative Consultants, Inc., (ICI) an Illinois "C" corporation, based in Washington DC, was founded by Donald M. Berlin on December 12, 1978. ICI started its operations as a general investigations firm for attorneys specializing in complex federal litigation and commercial transactions.

Investigative Consultants, Inc. specializes in providing computerized on-line database investigations and intelligence analysis through a worldwide network of computerized on databases that it is licensed to access. Each database has millions of files, and ICI subscribes to over 9,000 database services worldwide. Most of these databases are used to obtain in-depth background information on people, organizations, institutions, and corporations for attorneys and multinational corporations. ICI currently offers it services only to licensed attorneys, law firms, or attorneys that work for multi-national corporations.

Special emphasis is placed on:

- International corporate due-diligence investigations.

- Complex litigation management and strategy services, using databases to conduct difficult investigations quickly and efficiently.

- Venture capital and banking due-diligence investigation on individuals in 122 countries.

23

Privileged and Confidential – Attorney Work Product –

- Tracing of assets, banking, financial and credit investigations because of defaults and other losses.

- Estate preservation searches done by trustees to protect erosion of principal by unknown persons.

- High-level pre-employment background searches on executives.

ICI is capable of conducting these and others kinds of inquiries and presenting a highly proprietary report format because of its unique methods and sources.

ICI uses experts in litigation management and administration with 25 years' experience in intelligence gathering, data interpretations, and criminal investigations; professionals in psychology and management-sciences who have testified throughout the country as expert witnesses in complex federal and state litigation; and outside contractors and staff members who have over 25 years of U.S. Foreign Service experience, specializing in overseas investigations and risk-analysis.

These specialists, combined with other experts who focus on the more technical assignments, enable ICI to evaluate large volumes of raw data for well-defined purposes. Thus, for example, it is possible to examine more than 50 categories of background information on prospective jurors, witnesses or experts, and alert counsel to character or personality traits indicated by these factors. Such an evaluation can help in developing trial tactics and in understanding the psychological receptivity of individual jurors to the case presented.

ICI brings together the combined and integrated senior staffs of two complementary organizations involved in data collection, research, and intelligence analysis. Both organizations have vast experience in litigation management, intelligence services and investigative research on a worldwide basis.

It may be necessary to conduct ground investigation in the US or some foreign country. Once the initial searches are done and ICI's intelligence analysts have reviewed them for additional leads, sources can be used to do follow-up investigation. However, ground investigation is not part of a standard proposal process.

ICI's network affiliates are former career Foreign Service officials in the United States and abroad that have worked in the field of counterintelligence, money laundering detection, and international finance.

As an outside purveyor of investigative services, ICI removes the client from direct involvement with sensitive inquiries. That is one reason ICI's client list includes many of America's largest and most prestigious law firms which have their own in-house electronic database capability. Among the advantages it offers, ICI:

- Constructs customized searches depending on the investigative objectives of counsel and the type of information that is needed.

- Conducts all inquiries, electronic and otherwise, on its own authority. The law firm client, and its ultimate client, is not identified with the investigation.

- Keeps abreast of new database sources used in all legal specialties. Furthermore, it constantly uses these sources and knows their capabilities from experience.

24

Privileged and Confidential — Attorney Work Product

- Expands to meet unusually complex or particularly urgent assignments, thus eliminating the need for the law firm client to strain its own staff resources.

- Combines electronic searches with necessary on-site investigations, when necessary. Performs at substantially lower overall cost for large investigations than does the law firm's in-house electronic library.

From 1989 to the present, ICI has researched, developed, and perfected several highly proprietary products and processes that are unique to the computerized on-line database industry. It has used these tools, combined with human assets, to provide corporations and law firms some of the finest intelligence products available in the private sector.

Privileged and Confidential - Attorney Work Product

b6
b7C

From:
Sent: Tue 8/04/2015 11:17 AM (GMT-04:00)
To: Steve Bannon
Cc:
Bcc:
Subject: [No Subject]

Corey just confirmed green light on Trump :-)))

US Cell:
UK Cell

CA Cambridge Analytica
The News Corp. Building, Suite 2703,
1211 Avenue of the Americas,
New York, NY 10036
Phone: +1 (646) 892-9591
www.cambridgeanalytica.org

14

From: Steve Bannon ▮▮▮▮▮▮▮▮ on behalf of Steve Bannon   **b6**
Sent: Sunday, June 12, 2016 02:01 PM   **b7C**
To: ▮▮▮▮▮▮▮▮
Cc:
Subject: Re: Defeat Crooked Hillary ▮▮▮▮

Love it   **b6**

On Jun 12, 2016, at 2:00 PM, ▮▮▮▮▮▮▮▮▮▮▮▮▮▮▮▮ wrote: **b7A**
     b7B per DOJ/OIP
Hi Steve,   **b7C**

When you are in the UK in the next fortnight, I think that we should meet with ▮▮▮▮
▮▮▮▮▮▮▮▮
▮▮▮▮▮▮▮▮ and I think that his input could be very
valuable for the Super PAC.

If you agree, we will try and connect with him.
(please remind me when you will be in London)

▮▮▮▮▮▮▮▮▮▮▮▮▮▮▮▮▮▮▮▮

▮   **b6**
     b7C

▮▮▮▮▮▮

US Cell ▮▮▮▮▮
UK Cell ▮▮▮▮▮▮▮

CA Cambridge Analytica
The News Corp. Building, Suite 2703
1211 Avenue of the Americas
New York, NY 10036
Phone: +1 (646) 892-9591

1 Wales Alley, Old Town
Alexandria, VA 22314
Phone: +1 (703) 997-1812

55 New Oxford Street
London, WC1A 1BS
Phone: +44 (0)20 3828 7529

http://cambridgeanalytica.org

1

From:
Sent: Sun 6/12/2016 2:00 PM (GMT-04:00)
To: Steve Bannon
Cc:
Bcc:
Subject: Defeat Crooked Hillary | Assange

Hi Steve,

When you are in the UK in the next fortnight, I think that we should meet with [redacted] and I think that his input could be very valuable for the Super PAC.

If you agree, we will try and connect with him.
(please remind me when you will be in London)

US Cell:
UK Cell:

CA Cambridge Analytica
The News Corp. Building, Suite 2703
1211 Avenue of the Americas
New York, NY 10036
Phone: +1 (646) 892-9591

1 Wales Alley, Old Town
Alexandria, VA 22314
Phone: +1 (703) 997-1812

55 New Oxford Street
London, WC1A 1BS
Phone: +44 (0)20 3828 7529

http://cambridgeanalytica.org

b6
b7C

b6
b7A
b7B per DOJ/OIP
b7C

b6
b7C

15

From: [redacted]   **b6**
To: Steve Bannon [redacted]   **b7A**
           [redacted]   **b7B per DOJ/OIP**
           [redacted]   **b7C**
Cc:
Bcc:
Subject: Data Guy in Trump Tower
Date: Thu Jan 07 2016 21:15:04 EST
Attachments:

[redacted] has been there six weeks. Does voter lists and call centers.

Sent from my BlackBerry 10 smartphone.

From:	Steve Bannon	**b6**
To:		**b7A**
		b7B per DOJ/OIP
Cc:		**b7C**
Bcc:		
Subject:		
Date:	Fri Aug 26 2016 13:18:53 EDT	
Attachments:		

Can u talk

Have some ideas

From:	Ted Malloch	b6
To:		b7A
		b7B per DOJ/OIP
Cc:		b7C
Bcc:		
Subject:	The Debate	
Date:	Tue Aug 30 2016 16:02:37 EDT	
Attachments:		

Steve,

As you well know from all my op-eds (some of which ran in Breitbart) and strategy pieces, I have been labouring non stop for the Trump campaign — even though I am all the way over here in Oxford. Please let me know if you need anything else or if I can be of further service.

I am back in the US speaking in Boston, Maryland, and LA in mid-October, to conservative and business audiences and will keep plugging.

b6
b7A
b7B per DOJ/OIP
b7C

I have been in constant touch with the campaign,

I have a clever idea for you and Donald for the first debate I wanted to pass along. I know you are in the preparation stage and hopefully will let him be himself, authentic and not overly scripted. Leave that to his inept opponent.

Here is the idea:

In his opening remarks Scene One, in other words—hand Hillary a Writ of Indictment. Have it typed out and actually hand it physically to her.

What is INDICTMENT?

A written accusation of one or more persons of a crime or misdemeanour, presented to, and preferred upon oath or affirmation, by a grand jury legally convoked. Say this and then add, this Indictment is on behalf of all the American people since our Justice Department will not indict you due to crony politics, I present it to you formally here tonight, and serve you on behalf of ALL the American people for you undeniable crimes against America, destruction of evidence in the form of emails, and theft of funds to your own personal benefit and enrichment.

It would steal the show!!! And be the headline we want.

Ted Roosevelt Malloch

From:

To:

Cc:

Bcc:

Subject: [redacted] in Vegas

Date: Wed Oct 19 2016 13:30:33 EDT

Attachments:

Steve, I am told [redacted] is in Vegas and willing to play any role in debate activities that is helpful. Any interest in utilizing him? Our friend in FL is working hard on this. Best [redacted]

Sent from my iPhone

From:	Steve Bannon
To:	
Cc:	
Bcc:	
Subject:	
Date:	Sat Oct 22 2016 07:02:02 EDT
Attachments:	

b6
b7A
b7B per DOJ/OIP
b7C

[____] can u arrange for [____] to meet with [__] soonest in NYC

He is here today and back mid week

To:
From: b6
Sent: 2016-09-21T07:51:30-05:00   b7C
Importance: Normal
Subject: Fwd: Wikileaks
Received: 2016-09-21T07:51:32-05:00

Sent from my iPhone

Begin forwarded message:

From: Donald Trump Jr.   b6
Date: September 21, 2016 at 2:09:34 AM EDT   b7C
To: Steve
Bannon   Jared Kushner

Subject: Wikileaks

Guys I got a weird Twitter DM from wikileaks. See below. I tried the password
and it works and the about section they reference contains the next pic in terms of
who is behind it. Not sure if this is anything but it seems like it's really wikileaks
asking me as I follow them and it is a DM. Do you know the people mentioned
and what the conspiracy they are looking for could be? These are just screen shots
but it's a fully built out page claiming to be a PAC let me know your thoughts and
if we want to look into it.

D

To: Steve Bannon
From: Jared Kushner
Sent: 2016-09-28T06:31:25-05:00
Importance: Normal
Subject: Re: request from the ft
Received: 2016-09-28T06:31:24-05:00

She is playing commercials about DJT's ties to oligarchs. Saying that is why he sint releasing his taxes

From: Steve Bannon
Date: Wednesday, September 28, 2016 at 7:16 AM
To: Michael Cohen
Cc: Kellyanne Conway   Jared
                                                        Stephen
Miller
Subject: Re: request from the ft

???

On Sep 28, 2016, at 6:09 AM, Michael Cohen   wrote:

> Sergei acknowledges that there has never been a relationship between him and the
> boss. Heir commercials are bogus and should be debunked.

Sent from my iPhone

Michael D. Cohen
Executive Vice President and
Special Counsel to
Donald J. Trump
725 Fifth Avenue
New York, New York 10022
Phone:
Cellular:

Begin forwarded message:

From: Sergio Millian
Date: September 27, 2016 at 2:48:40 PM EDT
To: Michael Cohen
Subject: Fwd: request from the ft

FYI

---------- Forwarded message ----------
From: Sergio Millian
Date: Tue, Sep 27, 2016 at 9:35 PM
Subject: Re: request from the ft

To: Catherine Belton

Catherine,

As I explained to you I have spoken to reporters in the past about Trump
and they misquoted me. I work with businesses from all over the world,
USA, EU, Africa, Russia, China, Japan, etc. I have a solid reputation with
businesses around the world. I am US citizen and do not have and never
had Russian citizenship. If you libel or slander my name and it hurts my
business, I will consult a lawyer.

Here are the answers to your questions.

I have never said that I worked personally for Mr Trump. I said I was a
broker for one of his many real estate projects. There are several brokers
who work on such real estate projects. I never represented Mr Trump
personally and I am not working with Mr Trump. I've never received a dime
from Mr. Trump. I have never been paid by Mr. Trump for any work. I have
never consulted Mr Trump on any political topics. I have never met Carter
Page. I am shocked to see my name used in press about the totally legal
real estate transactions and amounts that are of public knowledge in the
USA such as this one http://money.cnn.com/2016/07/27/news/donald-trump-
russian-deal-mansion/

How often do you speak with Mr. Trump? When was the last time? Eight
years ago (2008)

Thank you for honest reporting.

S

Best wishes,

Catherine

On 26 September 2016 at 21:36, Sergio Millian
_____ wrote:

Hello Catherine,

I saw you called me. I'm currently very busy with my business
projects. For some reason over 20 journalists called me during the
last 3 days.

Best regards,
Sergei

On 22 September 2016 at 03:13, Sergio Millian

[REDACTED] wrote:

Catherine,

For the record, all of the opinions and views expressed below are my personal views and not official views of the Chamber of Commerce or any of its members, clients or sponsors.

Has there been a slowdown in business deals between Russia and the US in the wake of sanctions and the standoff over Ukraine, or are in fact deals warming up now that there may be a chance of a Trump presidency and a more pro-Russian stance?

Yes, there has been a significant slowdown in NEW business deals between Russia and the US as a result of the sanctions.

What is the role of the Russian American Chamber of Commerce in fostering better ties?

The Russian American Chamber of Commerce in the USA is one of the main business organizations in the USA that assists U.S. companies in Russian and CIS markets entry. We primarily focus on assistance to U.S. manufacturers and exporters. We hosted five Export to Russia Forums with assistance from U.S. Commercial Service in the United States. The Chamber provides market information, practical advice, leads, and referrals to U.S. members of all sizes to facilitate U.S. export, distribution channels, and other forms of business development in Russia and the CIS countries. The Chamber may also assists U.S. members in obtaining visas, legal advice, translations, certifications, exhibition information, office space, HR-services, and offers a cultural program in the CIS. The Chamber facilitates cooperation for U.S. members with American corporations already working in Russia and CIS countries, the Russian Government, Russian Regional Administrations, U.S. Consulates in Russia, Chambers of Commerce in Russia, and corporate leaders from CIS countries.

Business-wise, despite sanctions, the relations between the USA are still quite strong(primarily because of old connections, previously signed contracts and favorable business climate built by President Obama during his first term in the White House when he made a genuine effort to reset the relationship with the Russians). I estimate there are currently more than 10,000 mainly small and medium size businesses businesses in our two countries, employing up to 3 million people.

One of the major goals of the United Nations and all peace-loving people is to stop the perpetual world war, which occurs in various forms on our planet for thousands of years, to stop and move in the direction of international cooperation. The only alternative to the global confrontation of civilizations, beliefs, religions, is the mutually beneficial economic cooperation of all countries.

Preventive military aggression, regime change, political pressure and economic war between the two countries and corporations are instruments of politically weak minds. Strong policy minds will create the necessary economic conditions for the prosperity in the United States and abroad.

Today, the world is again at a crossroads. For the hundredth time in human history. Again, as has already happened many times before, the world is experiencing economic, political, religious and phycological shock. It is high time to think again and stop grabbing the biggest piece of the pie. The global pie is huge, the wealth is so tremendous, there will be enough for all, if we excercise a reasonable approach to the planet's resources, and thoughtfully enjoy the benefits that God has given us.

Let's convert the energy of the global warming of the planet to the warming energy in human relations, employing the achievements in medical technology, information technology, construction, clean and efficient energy to the benefit of Mankind. Therefore, I can say that the responsibility for the future of the world rests upon all of us. It depends on scientists and businessmen, journalists and public workers, politicians and military. It entirely depends on us where our efforts will be directed in our daily business. I hope that the future president of the United States will spread her/his influence throughout the world in order to create global prosperity.

Best regards,
Sergei Millian

Message

From:	Steve Bannon
Sent:	11/5/2016 10:43:25 PM
To:	Jared Kushner · David Bossie
Subject:	Re: Securing the Victory

We need to avoid this guy like the plague

They are going to try and say the Russians worked with wiki leaks to give this victory to us

Paul is nice guy but can't let word get out he is advising us

Get Outlook for iOS

From: Jared Kushner
Sent: Saturday, November 5, 2016 5:39:20 PM
To: Steve Bannon; David Bossie
Subject: FW: Securing the Victory

What do u think?

From: Paul Manafort
Date: Saturday, November 5, 2016 at 11:36 AM
To: Jared
Subject: Securing the Victory

Jared
Not certain if you are offline but am sending for when you are online again.
I am really feeling good about our prospects on Tuesday and focusing on preserving the victory. This memo deals with this concern.
I sent this to Reince, and briefed Rick Gates and Hannity.
Good luck. We are almost there.
Paul

From: ⬛
Sent: Wed 4/20/2016 8:21 PM (GMT-04:00)
To: Steve Bannon
Cc: ⬛
Bcc:
Subject: Re: Cambridge Analytica

Hi ⬛
A pleasure to meet you. Is there a best time to call you tomorrow please?
⬛

Sent from my iPhone

> On 20 Apr 2016, at 20:00, Steve Bannon ⬛ wrote:
>
> ⬛ the company

b6
b7A
b7B per DOJ/OIP
b7C

From:
Sent: Wed 5/04/2016 8:13 AM (GMT-04:00)
To: Steve Bannon
Cc:
Bcc:
Subject: [No Subject]

TEXT RECEIVED FROM

I know   well - he is a total pretender!
We worked on our very first pilot program in Virginia with him in 2013

I will connect with him directly.

US Cell:
UK Cell

CA Cambridge Analytica
The News Corp. Building, Suite 2703,
1211 Avenue of the Americas,
New York, NY 10036
Phone: +1 (646) 892-9591

1 Wales Alley, Old Town,
Alexandria, VA 22314
Phone: +1 (703) 997-1812

1-6 Yarmouth Place, Mayfair,
London W1J 7BU   United Kingdom
Phone : +44(0)207 930 3500
www.cambridgeanalytica.org

This email is confidential and may be privileged. If you are not the intended recipient or have received this email in error, please notify the sender immediately and delete this email. Any unauthorized copying, disclosure or distribution of the material in this email is strictly forbidden. Please note that any views or opinions presented in this email are solely those of the author and do not necessarily represent those of the company. Finally, the recipient should check this email and any attachments for the presence of viruses. The company accepts no liability for any damage caused by any virus transmitted by this email.

Please consider the environment before printing this e-mail

b7E

FD-302 (Rev. 5-8-10)

FEDERAL BUREAU OF INVESTIGATION

Date of entry   09/06/2018

(U) MICHAEL DEAL COHEN (COHEN), date of birth [   ] was interviewed   b6
in the Special Counsel's Office, located at 395 E Street SE, Washington,   b7C
DC. COHEN was accompanied by his attorneys, Guy Petrilo, Amy Lester, and
Philip Pilmar, from the law offices of Petrilo Klein & Boxer LLP, 655
Third Avenue, New York, NY. Participating in the interview were FBI
Special Agent (SA) [   ] SA [   ]
Intelligence Analyst (IA) [   ] Forensic Accountant (FoA)
[   ] Senior Assistant Special Counsel (SASC) Jeannie S. Rhee,
SASC Andrew D. Goldstein, and Assistant Special Counsel L. Rush Atkinson.
Pursuant to signing a proffer agreement and after being advised of the
identity of the interviewing agents, COHEN provided the following
information:

b5 Per DOJ/OIP

b5 Per DOJ/OIP

b5 Per DOJ/OIP

Investigation on 08/07/2018 at Washington, District Of Columbia, United States (In Person)

File # [   ]   Date drafted 08/08/2018   b6
   b7C
by [   ]   b7E

FBI(19cv1278)-424

b5 Per DOJ/OIP

b5 Per DOJ/OIP

b6
b7C

b5 Per DOJ/OIP

b5 Per DOJ/OIP

b5 Per DOJ/OIP

b5 Per DOJ/OIP

b5 Per DOJ/OIP

b5 Per DOJ/OIP

b5 Per DOJ/OIP

b6
b7C

b5 Per DOJ/OIP

b5 Per DOJ/OIP

b6
b7A
b7C

b5 Per DOJ/OIP

b5 Per DOJ/OIP

b5 Per DOJ/OIP

b5 Per DOJ/OIP

b5 Per DOJ/OIP

TRUMP JUNIOR said to TRUMP that he was setting up a meeting in order to get dirt on HILLARY CLINTON. (COHEN did not recall whether TRUMP JUNIOR said "Clinton" or "Hillary.")

b5 Per DOJ/OIP

b5 Per DOJ/OIP

b5 Per DOJ/OIP

b5 Per DOJ/OIP

b5 Per DOJ/OIP

(U) Regarding the timing of the meeting, COHEN thought it was prior to
June 9th, 2016 by a couple of days   b5 Per DOJ/OIP

b6
b7C

COHEN reviewed
a calendar of June 2016 and estimated the conversation he witnessed
between TRUMP JUNIOR and TRUMP was Monday, June 6, 2016,

b5 Per DOJ/OIP

b5 Per DOJ/OIP

b5 Per DOJ/OIP

b5 Per DOJ/OIP

b5 Per DOJ/OIP

b6
b7C
b7A

b7E

FD-302a (Rev. 05-08-10)

b5 Per DOJ/OIP

b7A

b5 Per DOJ/OIP

b5 Per DOJ/OIP

b5 Per DOJ/OIP

b5 Per DOJ/OIP

b5 Per DOJ/OIP
b6
b7A
b7B Per DOJ/OIP
b7C

b5 Per DOJ/OIP

b6
b7A
b7B Per DOJ/OIP
b7C

b5 Per DOJ/OIP

b6
b7A
b7B Per DOJ/OIP
b7C

b5 Per DOJ/OIP

b6
b7A
b7B Per DOJ/OIP
b7C

COHEN heard   b5 Per DOJ/OIP
b7A
b7B Per DOJ/OIP
b7C
TRUMP said, "oh good, alright."

b5 Per DOJ/OIP

b6
b7A
b7B Per DOJ/OIP
b7C

bb5 Per DOJ/OIP
b7A
b7B Per DOJ/OIP
b7C

b5 Per DOJ/OIP

b6
b7A
b7B Per DOJ/OIP
b7C

b5 Per DOJ/OIP

b6
b7A
b7B Per DOJ/OIP
b7C

b5 Per DOJ/OIP

b6
b7A
b7B Per DOJ/OIP
b7C

b5 Per DOJ/OIP

b6
b7A
b7B Per DOJ/OIP
b7C

b5 Per DOJ/OIP

b6
b7A
b7B Per DOJ/OIP
b7C

b5 Per DOJ/OIP

b6
b7A
b7B Per DOJ/OIP
b7C

b5 Per DOJ/OIP

b5 Per DOJ/OIP

b6
b7A
b7B Per DOJ/OIP
b7C

b5 Per DOJ/OIP

b6
b7C

b5 Per DOJ/OIP

b5 Per DOJ/OIP

b6
b7C

b5 Per DOJ/OIP

b5 Per DOJ/OIP

b6
b7C

b5 Per DOJ/OIP

b5 Per DOJ/OIP

b5 Per DOJ/OIP

b5 Per DOJ/OIP

b5 Per DOJ/OIP

b5 Per DOJ/OIP

b5 Per DOJ/OIP

b5 Per DOJ/OIP

b5 Per DOJ/OIP

b5 Per DOJ/OIP

b5 Per DOJ/OIP

b5 Per DOJ/OIP

b5 Per DOJ/OIP

b5 Per DOJ/OIP

b6
b7C

b5 Per DOJ/OIP

b5 Per DOJ/OIP

b5 Per DOJ/OIP

b5 Per DOJ/OIP

(U) COHEN did not have discussions with the TRUMP CAMPAIGN about TTM.

b5 Per DOJ/OIP

(U) Nobody from the campaign asked COHEN how TTM was going.

b5 Per DOJ/OIP

b5 Per DOJ/OIP

b5 Per DOJ/OIP

b5 Per DOJ/OIP

b6
b7C

b5 Per DOJ/OIP

b5 Per DOJ/OIP

b5 Per DOJ/OIP

b5 Per DOJ/OIP

b6
b7C

b5 Per DOJ/OIP

b5 Per DOJ/OIP

COHEN knew he w b5 Per DOJ/OIP
Russian Olympic Weightlifter.

b5 Per DOJ/OIP

b5 Per DOJ/OIP

FD-302a (Rev. 05-08-10)

Continuation of FD-302 of (U) Interview of Michael Cohen , On 08/07/2018 , Page 18 of 22

b5 Per DOJ/OIP

b5 Per DOJ/OIP

b6
b7C

b5 Per DOJ/OIP

b5 Per DOJ/OIP

b7A

b5 Per DOJ/OIP

b6
b7C

b5 Per DOJ/OIP

b6
b7A
b7B Per DOJ/OIP
b7C

Continuation of FD-302 of (U) Interview of Michael Cohen _____ . On 08/07/2018 . Page 19 of 22

b5 Per DOJ/OIP

b7A

b5 Per DOJ/OIP

b6
b7C

b5 Per DOJ/OIP

b5 Per DOJ/OIP

b5 Per DOJ/OIP

b6
b7C

FD-302a (Rev. 05-08-10)

Continuation of FD-302 of <u>(U) Interview of Michael Cohen</u> , On <u>08/07/2018</u> , Page <u>20</u> of 22

b5 Per DOJ/OIP

b6
b7C

b5 Per DOJ/OIP

b6
b7C

b5 Per DOJ/OIP

b5 Per DOJ/OIP

b6
b7C

b5 Per DOJ/OIP

b6
b7C

b5 Per DOJ/OIP

b6
b7C

b5 Per DOJ/OIP

b5 Per DOJ/OIP

b5 Per DOJ/OIP

b6
b7C

b7E

b5 Per DOJ/OIP

b6
b7C

b5 Per DOJ/OIP

b6
b7C

b5 Per DOJ/OIP

b6
b7C

b5 Per DOJ/OIP

8/7/2018

Michael Cohen   attys: · Guy Patrilo   Petrilo Klein &
                              · Amy Lester   Boxer LLP,
                              · Philip Pilmar   655 Third Ave
                                                     New York, NY
LRA
JSR
ADG

b6
b7C

b5 Per DOJ/OIP

LRA:

b5 Per DOJ/OIP

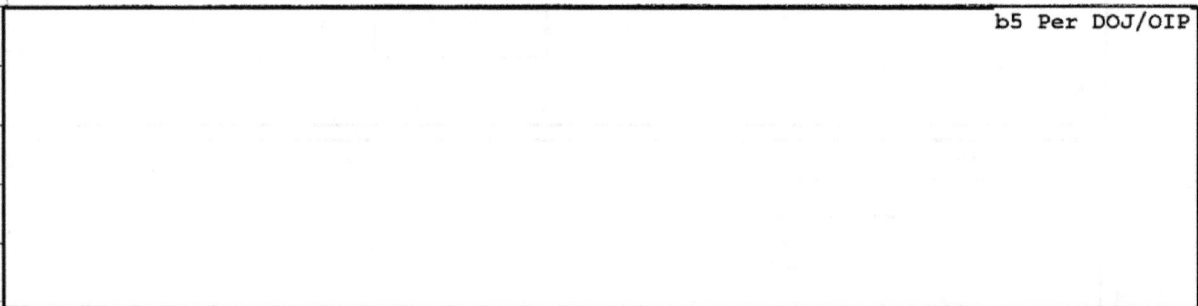

LRA

b5 Per DOJ/OIP

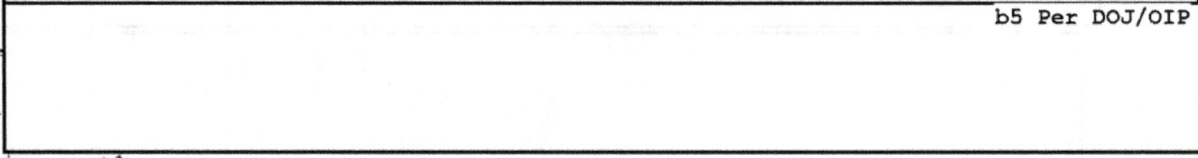

b5 Per DOJ/OIP

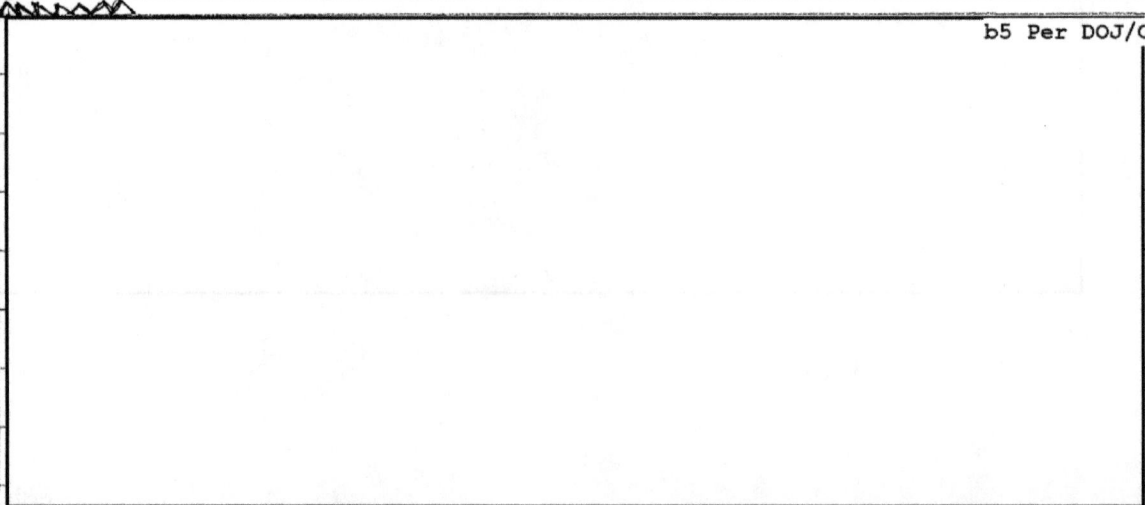

FBI(19cv1278)-446

b5 Per DOJ/OIP

DJT Jr : ~~Nothin~~
I have a meeting in order to get dirt
on Clinton.
 (or "Hillary")

b5 Per DOJ/OIP

prior to June 9 by a couple of days.
Rem. it was kind of the beginning of June

b5 Per DOJ/OIP

b6
b7C

b5 Per DOJ/OIP

b5 Per DOJ/OIP

b5 Per DOJ/OIP

b6
b7A
b7B Per DOJ/OIP
b7C

b5 Per DOJ/OIP

b6
b7A
b7B Per DOJ/OIP
b7C

I'll marcl

b5 Per DOJ/OIP

b6
b7A
b7B Per DOJ/OIP
b7C

DT - "oh good alright"

b5 Per DOJ/OIP

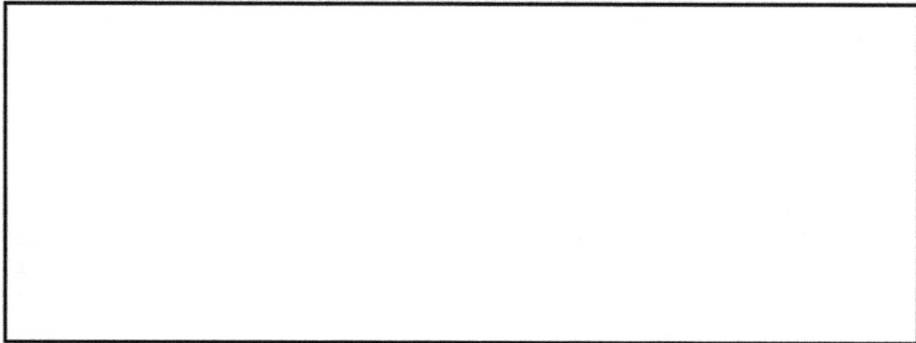

b5 Per DOJ/OIP

b5 Per DOJ/OIP

Any discussion w/ DOT org or campaign
abt TTPs at Same time at campaign
NO —

b5 Per DOJ/OIP

LPA

FBI(19cv1278)-481

Nobody asked how TPM was doing
in the context of campaign.

MC

FS

JSR

b5 Per DOJ/OIP

b5 Per DOJ/OIP

b6
b7C

b5 Per DOJ/OIP

Klokov —

b5 Per DOJ/OIP

Russn Olympic weight-lifter

ADG

MC

not at
Maralago

U.S. Department of Justice
The Special Counsel's Office

Washington, D.C. 20530

August 6, 2018

Guy Petrillo
Petrillo Klein & Boxer LLP
655 Third Ave.
22nd Floor
New York, NY 10017

Re: Michael D. Cohen

Dear Counsel:

You have indicated that your client Michael D. Cohen (hereinafter "Client"), is interested in providing information to the government.

With respect to the meeting between the government, Client and yourself on August 7, 2018 (hereinafter "the meeting"), the government will be represented by individuals from the Special Counsel's Office and the Federal Bureau of Investigation. The terms of this letter do not bind any office or component of the U.S. Department of Justice other than those identified in the preceding sentence. The following terms and conditions apply to the meeting:

(1)   **THIS IS NOT A COOPERATION AGREEMENT.** Client has agreed to provide information to the government, and to respond to questions truthfully and completely. By receiving Client's proffer, the government does not agree to make any motion on Client's behalf or to enter into a cooperation agreement, plea agreement, immunity agreement or non- prosecution agreement with Client. The government makes no representation about the likelihood that any such agreement will be reached in connection with this meeting.

(2)   Should Client be prosecuted, no statements made by Client during the meeting will be used against Client in the government's case-in-chief at trial or for purposes of sentencing, except as provided below.

(3)   The government may use any statement made or information provided by Client, or on Client's behalf, in a prosecution for false statements, perjury, or obstruction of justice, premised on statements or actions during the meeting. The government may also use any such statement or information at sentencing in support of an argument that Client failed to provide truthful or complete information during the meeting, and, accordingly: (a) that under the United States Sentencing Guidelines, Client is not entitled to a downward adjustment for acceptance of

responsibility pursuant to Section 3E1.1, or should receive an upward adjustment for obstruction of justice pursuant to Section 3C1.1; and (b) that Client's conduct at the meeting is a relevant factor under 18 U.S.C. § 3553(a).

(4) The government may make derivative use of any statements made or other information provided by Client during the meeting. Therefore, the government may pursue any investigative leads obtained directly or indirectly from such statements and information and may use the evidence or information subsequently obtained therefrom against Client in any manner and in any proceeding.

(5) In any proceeding, including sentencing, the government may use Client's statements and any information provided by Client during or in connection with the meeting to cross- examine Client, to rebut any evidence or arguments offered on Client's behalf, or to address any issues or questions raised by a court on its own initiative.

(6) Neither this agreement nor the meeting constitutes a plea discussion or an attempt to initiate plea discussions. In the event this agreement or the meeting is later construed to constitute a plea discussion or an attempt to initiate plea discussions, Client knowingly and voluntarily waives any right Client might have under Fed. R. Evid. 410, Fed. R. Crim. P. 11(f), or otherwise, to prohibit the use against Client of statements made or information provided during the meeting.

(7) The government reserves the right to argue that neither this agreement nor the meeting constitutes the timely provision of complete information to the government concerning Client's involvement in an offense, within the meaning of Section 3E1.l(b) of the Sentencing Guidelines.

(8) If and when required to do so by a court, the government may disclose to the Probation Office or the court any statements and information provided by Client during the meeting.

(9) The government may disclose the fact of the meeting or the information provided by Client during the meeting to the extent the government determines in its sole discretion that disclosure would be in furtherance of its discharge of its duties and responsibilities or is otherwise required by law. Such disclosure includes disclosure to a local, state, federal, or foreign government office or agency, including but not limited to another prosecutor's office, if the recipient of the information agrees to abide by the relevant terms of this agreement.

(10) The terms and conditions set forth in this agreement extend, if applicable, to the continuation of the meeting on the dates that appear below.

(11) It is understood that this agreement is limited to the statements made by Client at the meeting and does not apply to any oral, written or recorded statements made by Client at any other time.

(12) This document embodies the entirety of the agreement between the government and Client to provide information and evidence. No other promises, agreements or understandings exist between Client and the government regarding Client's provision of information or evidence

to the government.

(13)   Client and Client's attorney acknowledge that they have read, fully discussed and understand every paragraph and clause in this document and the consequences thereof.

Dated: _August 7, 2018_

At: _Washington, DC_

ROBERT S. MUELLER, III
Special Counsel

By: L. Rush Atkinson
Assistant Special Counsel
The Special Counsel's Office

Michael D. Cohen

Guy Petrillo
Attorney for Client

Dates of Continuation   Initials of counsel, Client and government attorney

_____   _____

_____   _____

_____   _____

www.ingramcontent.com/pod-product-compliance
Lightning Source LLC
Chambersburg PA
CBHW061758260326
41914CB00006B/1150